Intimate Letters from Petrograd

AMERICANS IN REVOLUTIONARY RUSSIA

Vol. 1
Albert Rhys Williams, *Through the Russian Revolution*, edited by
William Benton Whisenhunt (2016)

Vol. 2
Princess Julia Cantacuzène, Countess Spéransky, née Grant, *Russian People: Revolutionary Recollections*, edited by Norman E. Saul (2016)

Vol. 3
Ernest Poole, *The Village: Russian Impressions*, edited by Norman E. Saul (2017)

Vol. 4
John Reed, *Ten Days That Shook the World*, edited by
William Benton Whisenhunt (2017)

Vol. 5
Louise Bryant, *Six Red Months in Russia*, edited by Lee A. Farrow (2017)

Vol. 6
Edward Alsworth Ross, *Russia in Upheaval*, edited by Rex A. Wade (2017)

Vol. 7
Donald Thompson, *Donald Thompson in Russia*, edited by David H. Mould (2018)

Vol. 8
Arthur Bullard, *The Russian Pendulum: Autocracy—Democracy—Bolshevism*,
edited by David W. McFadden (2019)

Vol. 9
Pauline S. Crosley, *Intimate Letters from Petrograd*, edited by Lee A. Farrow (2019)

Vol. 10
"The Bolshevik Revolution Had Descended on Me": Madeleine Z. Doty's Russian Revolution,
edited by Julia L. Mickenberg (2019)

Vol. 11
David R. Francis, *Russia from the American Embassy*, edited by Vladimir V. Noskov (2019)

Series General Editors:
Norman E. Saul and William Benton Whisenhunt

Intimate Letters from Petrograd

Pauline S. Crosley

Edited and Introduction by
Lee A. Farrow

Anthem Press
An imprint of Wimbledon Publishing Company
www.anthempress.com

First published by Slavica Publishers, Indiana University, USA, 2019

This edition first published in UK and USA 2026
by ANTHEM PRESS
75–76 Blackfriars Road, London SE1 8HA, UK
or PO Box 9779, London SW19 7ZG, UK
and
244 Madison Ave #116, New York, NY 10016, USA

Copyright © 2026 Lee A. Farrow editorial matter and selection;
individual chapters © individual contributors

The moral right of the authors has been asserted.

All rights reserved. Without limiting the rights under copyright reserved above,
no part of this publication may be reproduced, stored or introduced into
a retrieval system, or transmitted, in any form or by any means
(electronic, mechanical, photocopying, recording or otherwise),
without the prior written permission of both the copyright
owner and the above publisher of this book.

British Library Cataloguing-in-Publication Data
A catalogue record for this book is available from the British Library.

Library of Congress Cataloging-in-Publication Data
A catalog record for this book has been requested.

ISBN-13: 978-1-83999-744-0 (Hbk)
ISBN-10: 1-83999-744-3 (Hbk)

ISBN-13: 978-1-83999-745-7 (Pbk)
ISBN-10: 1-83999-745-1 (Pbk)

Cover design: Tracey Theriault

Cover image courtesy of Minnetrista Heritage Collection, Muncie, Indiana.

This title is also available as an eBook.

CONTENTS

Editor's Introduction   vii
    Lee A. Farrow

Editor's Note   xvii

Acknowledgments   xix

INTIMATE LETTERS FROM PETROGRAD

Preface   3

I. The Siberian Railway   5

II. Petrograd   11

III. The Root Commission   33

IV. A Revolution!   43

V. After the Revolution   52

VI. Riga Captured   67

VII. Another Revolution   73

VIII. The Bolshevik Revolution	93
IX. Exit from Finland	126
Afterword	134
Appendix	139
Index	147

EDITOR'S INTRODUCTION
Lee A. Farrow

In late February 1917, while Russia was still embroiled in World War I, riots and demonstrations broke out in the capital city of Petrograd. These demonstrations were spontaneous and unexpected, but when the government attempted to disperse the crowds with reserve battalions, the soldiers began to fraternize with the demonstrators, and there were no other troops in the city to call. With Tsar Nicholas II at the front, authority largely collapsed. Many officials went into hiding, and the population of Petrograd turned to the country's consultative assembly, the Duma, for leadership. Recognizing the potential danger in this situation, the tsar tried to dissolve the Duma from afar, but its members ignored his order, and on February 27, 1917, they created a Provisional Government. As these events unfolded, Nicholas attempted to return to Petrograd, but he was stranded by railroad strikes in the city of Pskov. There, faced with the realities already described, and aware that he no longer had the support of his army commanders, Nicholas abdicated the throne, both for himself and for his son, in favor of his brother Michael. When Michael failed to accept the throne with any decisiveness, the Romanov dynasty, which had lasted over 300 years, from 1613 to 1917, came to an end.[1]

The Provisional Government consisted mostly of Duma members and other officials from the more liberal and moderate parties. Since the Duma had ignored the tsar's order to disband, the Provisional Government technically had no legitimate authority. It was thus intended to be a transitional body, in office until a Constituent Assembly could be elected, and because of its temporary nature, it put off dealing with critical questions, the most important of these being land reform and the war. Throughout the summer of 1917, the Provisional Government more or less continued to pursue the same unsatisfactory policies. In late June and early July, it launched the last Russian offensive of World War I, an attack on Austro-German forces along a broad front in Galicia, which ultimately failed. This misstep resulted in more riots

---

[1] Sheila Fitzpatrick, *The Russian Revolution, 1917–1932* (Oxford: Oxford University Press, 1982), 34–60; Orlando Figes, *A People's Tragedy: The Russian Revolution, 1891–1924* (New York: Penguin Books, 1998), 310–51; Richard Pipes, *The Russian Revolution* (New York: Vintage, 1991), 272–337.

and a failed attempt to overthrow the Provisional Government by the Bolsheviks, a Marxist group led by Vladimir Lenin.[2]

Vladimir Lenin, the Marxist theorist and revolutionary who was eager to establish a workers' state, had over a number of years gathered a group of followers around him under the name of the Bolsheviks. When the Revolution broke out in February, Lenin was in exile in Switzerland. Writing from Switzerland, he made it clear that he opposed the Provisional Government and hoped to topple it; he also expressed his intent to take Russia out of the war. This last declaration of Lenin's meant that France and Italy, both allies of Russia, would not allow Lenin passage home. Germany, however, was more than happy to help him; the only condition was that he travel in a sealed train car so that he could not incite any workers' movements in Germany along the way. So Lenin, along with his wife and several associates, arrived in Petrograd in early April and began to persuade the other Bolsheviks in the worker's organization known as the Petrograd Soviet that it was time to stage the revolution. He explained his program for action, promising to accomplish three things once he had control of the government: to take Russia out of the war, to distribute land to the peasantry, and to give workers control over the factories. It was, of course, these things which the Provisional Government refused to do, and this would ultimately result in its downfall.[3]

In the next months, the Provisional Government faced challenges it simply could not overcome. In early September there was an attempt to overthrow the government by a Russian military commander, Lavr Kornilov. Though the coup was stopped, the Provisional Government came out of the crisis looking weaker than before, while the position of the Bolsheviks was greatly strengthened. In fact, it was their leadership in putting down the attempted coup which gave them the strength and popularity to finally win control of both the Petrograd and Moscow Soviets.[4] Finally, in October, the Bolsheviks took action. On the night of October 24–25, the coup was carried out under Leon Trotsky's leadership, as the Petrograd Soviet's military arm, the Red Guard, seized the vital centers in Petrograd such as the telephone exchange, and electricity and railroad offices. The Provisional Government held out briefly in the Winter Palace, but its defenses were weak; the majority of the soldiers in Petrograd supported the Bolshevik takeover.[5] Lenin and the Bolsheviks now controlled the Russian capital and began to construct a communist system that would govern the nation

---

[2] Fitzpatrick, *The Russian Revolution*, 34–60; Figes, *A People's Tragedy*, 279–82, 421–38; Pipes, *The Russian Revolution*, 385–438.

[3] Fitzpatrick, *The Russian Revolution*, 34–60; Figes, *A People's Tragedy*, 384–87; Pipes, *The Russian Revolution*, 341–84.

[4] Fitzpatrick, *The Russian Revolution*, 34–60; Figes, *A People's Tragedy*, 451–61; Pipes, *The Russian Revolution*, 385–438.

[5] Figes, *A People's Tragedy*, 469–500; Pipes, *The Russian Revolution*, 439–505.

for most of the twentieth century. Pauline Stewart Crosley, author of *Intimate Letters from Petrograd*, was a witness to these dramatic events.

Pauline de Launay Stewart was born in Columbus, Georgia in 1871.[6] Though her early life remains obscure, she eventually attended Mary Baldwin College, an all-girls school in Staunton, Virginia, and graduated in 1885. Ten years later, Stewart married Walter Crosley in Annapolis, Maryland. Crosley was from East Jaffrey, New Hampshire, and had graduated from the US Naval Academy in 1893. In the navy, he served in a variety of positions, participating in the Sino-Japanese War, the Spanish-American War, and the American occupation of Haiti and Santo Domingo. Since most of this service was at sea, Pauline did not accompany her husband, but Walter visited home between assignments, and they had two sons between 1897 and 1902.[7] In early 1917, Walter was ordered to report as naval attaché to Petrograd, and this time, Pauline traveled with him. They arrived in Russia in April 1917.

Over the next eleven months, the Crosleys witnessed the last gasps of the Russian Empire and the emergence of the new Bolshevik-led communist regime. Crosley was sent to replace Newton McCully, who had been an observer in Russia of the Russo-Japanese War. Consequently, McCully was familiar with Russia and spoke the language fluently. Crosley, on the other hand, had no experience with Russia or its language, nor did his wife. Throughout this period, Pauline wrote letters describing the changing political landscape and the challenges of daily life in a city in the midst of, and in the wake of, revolution. Though her letters were written primarily to family members, when she chose to publish them in 1920, she recognized their potential value and the interest they might hold for a larger audience. In the foreword to her book, Crosley wrote, "May these letters now serve to interest and enlighten those others who would know what has not before been published!"

Crosley's book of published letters is an important and fascinating addition to the body of firsthand literature on the Russian Revolution. It is particularly important as the product of a female author. There were, in fact, a number of American women in Russia during the revolution who chronicled their experiences, but their writings have

---

[6] Her headstone at Arlington Cemetery says she was born in 1871, but census records accessed through ancestry.com show her as being two years old in 1870. At the same time, a passenger list from 1930 lists her as being fifty-seven years old, which would make her born in 1873.

[7] "Crosley, Walter Selwyn: rear admiral, U.S. Navy," *Who's Who in Government* (New York: Biographical Research Bureau, 1930).

often been overlooked or underappreciated. Many have likely heard of the American journalist and socialist John Reed and his celebrated book, *Ten Days That Shook the World*. Fewer, however, know of the contributions of his wife, Louise Bryant (played by Diane Keaton in "Reds," opposite Warren Beatty as Reed). A journalistic talent in her own right, Bryant published *Six Red Months in Russia* after returning from Russia, but her sex and her relationship with Reed overshadowed her talent as a writer and the depth of her observations of this historic event. Probably the second most well-known female chronicler of the revolution was Bessie Beatty, correspondent for the *San Francisco Bulletin*. In 1918, Beatty published her own account of the revolution, *The Red Heart of Russia*.

The observations of both Bryant and Beatty were well received at the time of their publication, but over time their accounts became largely forgotten. One possible reason for this was that these female interpretations of the revolution, in the words of one historian, did not "fit comfortably within the American narratives about the Russian Revolution." While the accounts by male observers concentrated on politics and military matters, those of their female counterparts tended to describe domestic concerns about the daily necessities of life, food and housekeeping matters, as well as "how both Russians and visiting Americans experienced grand historical events at the level of their quotidian existence." In doing so, women writers may have unwittingly contributed to the perception that their interpretations were less serious and informative. Nothing could be farther from the truth. Both Bryant and Beatty provided insights and details that male journalists ignored. They humanized the revolution, demonstrating that the larger proletariat was made of individual people, women and men, soldiers and returning émigrés. By largely focusing on the human angle, they reminded readers that the revolution was not simply a political upheaval but a traumatic disruption of ordinary life as well.[8]

Crosley's observations are both similar to and different from those of Bryant and Beatty. As journalists and feminists, Bryant and Beatty were often in the thick of things; they bravely ventured into the world of men, and their writings reflect this. Crosley, on the other hand, was in Russia as the wife of a diplomat and, consequently, her role dictated how much of the revolution she could witness and through what lens. Her world was smaller than that of her journalist contemporaries, her concerns more focused on her immediate surroundings and her circle of friends and acquaintances. Her letters are personal in nature, and give no indication that she relied upon the information being gathered by journalists like Reed, Bryant, or Beatty.

This is not to say, however, that a diplomat's wife was unimportant. In the first several decades of the twentieth century, American women played an important role in the US Foreign Service, accompanying their husbands at their diplomatic posts

---

[8] Choi Chatterjee, "'Odds and Ends of the Russian Revolution,' 1917–1920: Gender and American Travel Narratives," *Journal of Women's History* 20, 4 (2008): 12, 16–17.

around the world. Though the Foreign Service was adamant that women were not capable of serving in diplomatic roles themselves, it was widely understood that a man could potentially advance his career with a capable wife at his side. Diplomatic wives, in fact, were very busy women. In the words of one scholar, they "organized and managed social functions, packed and unpacked households, hired and fired servants, met new people, threw lavish dinner parties, volunteered in the local community, and learned new languages, customs, and rules of protocol all over the world."[9] They facilitated their husbands' careers in other ways as well. As they formed relationships with local women and other diplomatic wives, they participated in the exchange of information and the building of friendly relations. They viewed their husbands' profession as their own and took that responsibility very seriously. These wives understood that they were representing their husbands and their countries in all they did.[10]

Pauline Crosley's role and experience in Russia in 1917 was much the same as that of the diplomatic wives of the US Foreign Service. She was largely responsible for her family's social calendar and the day-to-day operations of their home. Her letters tend to focus on the details of everyday life, particularly the assessment of their fuel and food supplies. Crosley wrote to friends about the scarcity of fuel in middle of the Russian winter, declaring, "Our lamps keep us alive and we chase kerosene madly—candles are so scarce....We have double banked every stove daily and keep two kerosene stoves going day and night up to midnight and even then are only warm in rooms where small stoves burn."[11] The acquisition of good food was also a constant worry. In September 1917, Crosley observed, "Food is growing scarcer, the lines all longer...food riots will surely be here this winter."[12] Her fears about obtaining food grew with each passing month. In January 1918, two months after the revolution, Crosley expressed great concern about her diminishing food supply, crediting her husband with the forethought to stockpile supplies: "It is terrible these days. Thank fortune my husband was far seeing—we brought good food with us and his insistence a ship be sent has been a boon but in two months we will have nothing left of it.... Eggs can't be had. I bought 250 at a good sum, and still have one doz."[13]

One of the reasons Crosley focused on the need for adequate fuel supplies and "good food" is that she frequently threw teas and dinner parties at her home. These get-togethers were a regular feature of the social life of foreign diplomats in

---

[9] Molly M. Wood, "Wives, Clerks, and 'Lady Diplomats': The Gendered Politics of Diplomacy and Representation in the U.S. Foreign Service, 1900–1940," *European Journal of American Studies* 10, 1 (2015): 2.

[10] Ibid., 3.

[11] Pauline Crosley to Mrs. Smith, January 11, 1918, Crosley Collection, Harry Ransom Center, The University of Texas at Austin.

[12] Ibid., September 18, 1917, Crosley Collection.

[13] Ibid., January 11, 1918, Crosley Collection.

Petrograd, and Crosley enjoyed attending and hosting parties a great deal. Throughout her letters, she mentions social gatherings of various types and the people she met, which included humanitarian volunteers, businessmen, and diplomats from around the world, along with their wives and, sometimes, children. These parties served another function as well; they created a network of foreigners who could exchange information about where to obtain goods and who could assist in finding housing. The apartment that Crosley and her husband came to occupy in Petrograd was secured through one of these social connections. These parties also allowed foreigners in Russia to share rumors and stories about events in the city, violence on the streets, and the changing political situation. Crosley's letters frequently refer to incidents that she herself did not witness, but that she relays as truth. As a woman accompanying her husband, she did not have direct contact with the people or events that were changing the face of Russia the way Louise Bryant and Bessie Beatty did. Pauline Crosley had to rely on the news she received from her husband and the various social acquaintances she encountered through parties and her work at the American lazaret, a hospital established by the American colony in Petrograd to care for wounded soldiers and war refugees.

Information through unofficial sources was greatly valued because official information was difficult to obtain or entirely unreliable. Crosley frequently complained about the inability to receive trustworthy news. In November 1917, she wrote, "The Bolsheviks censor all reports. Telegrams are neither going nor coming as they should....To seek facts one must get them when possible from people who were on the spot and saw and heard much....It is simply <u>useless</u> to depend on newspapers."[14] At the same time, Crosley complained that American newspapers did not understand the events occurring in Russia and she wished she could write in and correct the misinformation being printed. She also was frustrated with the snail-like pace and the inconsistency of mail service; this was especially distressing to Crosley since her two sons were back in the United States, and though they were already young adults, she mentions concerns about insurance and education costs and the difficulty of managing those things from afar.

Crosley saw many other changes in Russia in the wake of the empire's collapse. She recounted the growing numbers of idle, roaming soldiers, and stories of violence in the streets. Over the course of the summer of 1917, she reported that the sound of gunfire became commonplace. Through friends and acquaintances she relayed accounts of random assaults and abuse. Often, Crosley's own background and position in society crept into her observations about the changes occurring in Russian life. In May 1917, for example, she bemoaned the declining atmosphere at the ballet performances that she attended and treasured so dearly, commenting, "The contrast between the former brilliant audience and the present somber one is brought to our

---

[14] Ibid., November 17, 1917, Crosley Collection.

attention by those who have lived a long while in Russia. Now, one sees soldiers, sailors and peasants occupying the Royal Box and there is none of the former brilliancy of smart gowns and gorgeous uniforms."[15] Later, she blames the revolution for the problems she has with one of her servants. In January 1918, she wrote, "Shocking and painful conditions in Russia and likely to grow worse during the coming months. Some day all may come right but class hatred is very intense and growing mutual. The servants everywhere are getting under the spell of the <u>independence</u> and disagreeable—I have been on the eve several times of sending this cook off—She has a beastly temper that caused my temper to fly loose today and I threatened her with dismissal."[16]

Crosley's assessment of the Russian people is often harsh. She expresses frustration with their passivity and complacency as the Russian Empire falls to pieces. She referred to Russia as "a country so pitifully without backbone, where the highest and the lowest are miserable and allow themselves to keep so."[17] Even as she lavishes praise on Russian cultural activities, describing her admiration for the Russian ballet, the Russian orchestra, and Russian church singing, she is a harsh critic of Russian common soldiers and Russian men in general, whom she often portrays as weak. Though Crosley knows little of Russia's history, she attempts to explain the origins of the February Revolution and the events that followed. She repeatedly refers to German involvement in the unfolding events in Russia and clearly believes that Lenin and the Bolsheviks were backed by and aided by German forces.

At the same time, Crosley is sympathetic to the Russian military officers of the old regime whose positions were swept away with the collapse of the monarchy. In the summer of 1917, she described the flood of Russian officers who approached her husband for help obtaining a position in the US military. Crosley noted, "It is difficult to convince them that our laws prevent what they desire, and while they cannot have their wish gratified one must be sorry for them. There is very little in sight for them in Russia; many of them come in disguise; they are in hiding because they were more or less prominent under the old regime and they would be killed or imprisoned if recognized now."[18]

On the night of the actual Bolshevik Revolution, Crosley was indoors, safely shielded from all the gunfire on the streets of the city, though she could hear cannon fire. She wrote to an acquaintance, "We are in the midst of another Bolshevik uprising. The city was taken on Wednesday night between ten and 3 a.m. So easy!"[19] Sev-

---

[15] Pauline Crosley, *Intimate Letters from Petrograd* (New York: E. P. Dutton, 1920).

[16] Pauline Crosley to Mrs. Smith, January 31, 1918, Crosley Collection.

[17] Ibid., January 11, 1918, Crosley Collection.

[18] Crosley, *Intimate Letters from Petrograd*, 45.

[19] Pauline Crosley to Mrs. Smith, November 10, 1917, Crosley Collection.

eral days later she and her husband walked to the site of the actual takeover, noting, "The Winter Palace looks as if it had smallpox. The windows on the side arch next to Nevsky area all shot out. The palace is peppered with bullets."[20] In subsequent days, she described the omnipresence of soldiers and the looting of various shops. She also noted that "the air for two or three blocks around the Palace is redolent with the fumes of the superior wines; the snow is stained and covered with broken bottles."[21] In the weeks after the revolution, Crosley reports the growing disrespect for foreigners, the confiscation of homes and material wealth from Russian nobility, and the increasing disorder on the city's streets.

Occasionally, her observations seem trite, such as when she complains about her difficulty in obtaining the appropriate ingredients for food for her dinner parties and teas. In December 1917, for example, Crosley noted the following event, with indignation that seems a bit misplaced: "Last Monday we awoke to the realization that all Switzars… and dvorniks in the city were on a strike, the same having been ordered by Smolney. Our dear old switzar is very sad—he does not want to strike; he is threatened with death if he works! The annoying part of it was that we were giving a dinner on Monday night and the front door was locked; the owner was afraid to open it. Our guests had to come in the back way, through the kitchen!" Similarly, in January 1918, Crosley wrote: "We have given two more large dinners, and have been out several times, but it is becoming a great effort to entertain *or* to be entertained. The streets are really not safe, and no one enjoys going out at night." Nonetheless, it is important to remember that Crosley was a dependent traveling with her husband, not a journalist, and so her role was of a more social nature. Given her reliance on these social interactions for news and acquiring goods, the difficulty to move freely between apartments would have been a limitation with genuine significance to her.

In early March 1918, the Crosleys left Petrograd. According to a letter of Walter Crosley, they had only eight hours' notice to pack their things and prepare to leave. Pauline describes packing all night, not only their belongings but also the belongings of the couple whose apartment they had been renting. She describes Walter's last minute rushing: "Getting tickets and passports under such a government is beyond words to describe what Walter Crosley was overwhelmed with. In an organized country you know where to go and what to do but in Petrograd under Red Guards I assure you it's the 7th Wonder of the World!" She and Walter made the best arrangements they could to protect the apartment and its contents from vandalism or theft after they left, leaving money to pay the rent and the servants for several months, and leaving food and fuel as well.[22] They then made a daring escape with a group of others via Finland, first by train then by sleigh. By this point, Russia was already descending into

---

[20] Ibid., November 17, 1917, Crosley Collection.

[21] Crosley, *Intimate Letters from Petrograd*, 233.

[22] Pauline Crosley to Mrs. Smith, March 5, 1918, Crosley Collection.

a civil war between pro-Bolshevik forces called "Reds" and the opposition known as the "Whites." Navigating their way across the dangerous Civil War front, the Crosleys encountered cold, hunger, and physical discomfort, but they finally made their way to Sweden. Her last letter that she chose to include in her book is from Sweden. It concludes with this appeal: "Before I end this I must put in one plea about that most horrible disease! *Please*, as you are a patriot, use every means within your power to prevent that disease from getting a start in the United States. There is no step too difficult to be well warranted, for the only cure for Bolshevism is death to it!"[23]

After departing Russia, the Crosleys lived in a number of other places as Walter served in different positions within the navy. Over the years, as Crosley traveled with her husband, she kept in contact with her alma mater, informing them of her travels and changing address.[24] Only a few years before her death, she contributed money to the alumnae fund.[25] Pauline Crosley died in 1955 and is buried along with her husband in Arlington Cemetery.

Despite some of their limitations, Crosley's letters are very interesting and distinct from other similar sources. Her descriptions of life in revolutionary St. Petersburg are told in dated letters, thus her impressions are fresh and immediate and resemble a diary or first-hand report. She was not a journalist or professional writer and has published nothing else that we know of, and while her letters may have been edited before publication, they do not appear significantly edited or polished, as is clear from the style of her writing and the frequent repetition. Finally, her correspondence spans a whole year, well into the Bolshevik period, which is atypical for the comparable memoirs and accounts that are available. Crosley's letters give us a sense of what life was like during these tumultuous months and serve as a fascinating companion to some of the more politically detailed accounts of the revolutionary period. Her frustration as Russia degenerates into chaos is real, as is her sense that intervention by either the Allies or an organized force of Russians might have prevented the Bolshevik takeover. Her focus on the toll which the revolution takes on Russian cultural life is a stark reminder of how political upheavals can, and often do, impact all aspects of a society. Similarly, Crosley's complaints about the difficulty of obtaining food, fuel, and reliable information highlight the ways in which the revolution affected everyday life for average Russian people. For most Russians, the challenge of day-to-day existence

---

[23] Crosley, *Intimate Letters from Petrograd*, 296.

[24] Mary Baldwin Bulletin Alumnae News Letter, January 1938, 21; Mary Baldwin Bulletin News Letter, March 1935, 29; Mary Baldwin News Letter, July 1929, 17; Mary Baldwin News Letter, April 1928.

[25] Mary Baldwin Alumnae News Letter, November 1952, 14.

would have been a greater concern than the details of the country's political turmoil, making Crosley's book a valuable resource for viewing the revolution from below.

Further Reading

Beatty, Bessie. *The Red Heart of Russia*. New York: Century, 1918.

Bryant, Louise. *Six Red Months in Russia*. Edited by Lee A. Farrow. Bloomington, IN: Slavica, 2017.

Figes, Orlando. *A People's Tragedy: The Russian Revolution, 1891–1924*. New York: Penguin Books, 1998.

Fitzpatrick, Sheila. *The Russian Revolution, 1917–1932*. Oxford: Oxford University Press, 1982.

Kennan, George F. *Russia and the West under Lenin and Stalin*. Boston: Little Brown, 1961.

Lieven, Dominic. *The End of Tsarist Russia: The March to World War I and Revolution*. New York: Viking, 2015.

Pipes, Richard. *The Russian Revolution*. New York: Vintage, 1991.

———. *Three Whys of the Russian Revolution*. New York: Vintage, 1995.

Pomper, Philip. *The Russian Revolutionary Intelligentsia*. Arlington Heights, IL: Harlan Davidson, 1970.

Reed, John. *Ten Days That Shook the World*. Edited by William Benton Whisenhunt. Bloomington, IN: Slavica, 2017.

Saul, Norman. *War and Revolution: The United States and Russia, 1914–1921*. Lawrence: University Press of Kansas, 2001.

Smith, S. A. *The Russian Revolution: A Very Short Introduction*. Oxford: Oxford University Press, 2002.

Wade, Rex A. *The Russian Revolution, 1917*. Cambridge: Cambridge University Press, 2000.

Weeks, Charles J. *An American Naval Diplomat in Revolutionary Russia: The Life and Times of Newton A. McCully*. Annapolis, MD: Naval Institute Press, 1993.

EDITOR'S NOTE

This republication of *Intimate Letters from Petrograd* contains all the text of the original publication, with the addition of an introduction for background and context and annotations to identify major people, places, and events. Crosley encountered many people during her time in Petrograd, and not all of them were of equal importance for our purposes or could be identified; those whose background was not essential to an understanding of the text or who could not be identified are marked with a question mark in brackets.

Some alterations have been made with regard to the spelling and transliteration of proper names of people and places. For example, Crosley usually spelled Russian family names with the ending "ff" instead of the more modern transliteration "v," and added an "e" to the end of Lenin's name. Moreover, she hyphenated words that we do not, such as "any-one," "some-one," and "no-one." These hyphens have all been removed.

Because Crosley's text here originally existed as letters, it often is broken into very short paragraphs, sometimes of only a sentence or two. In an effort to smooth out the text and make it more readable for a modern audience, the paragraphs have been combined and some reformatting has been employed.

ACKNOWLEDGMENTS

I would like to thank Ben Whisenhunt and Norman Saul for conceiving of this republication project and for all the hard work they have put into it, and Slavica for recognizing the usefulness of this series.

Though my children, Benjamin and Camille, may not realize it, they always inspire me to work hard and make them proud; they bring me more joy than they can ever know. Finally, I would like to thank Chris Bartlett, who helped me with some of my footnotes and who, for reasons that are beyond me, thinks that everything I do is fascinating and impressive.

Intimate Letters from Petrograd

BY

Pauline S. Crosley

Wife of a Temporary Diplomat

NEW YORK
E. P. DUTTON & COMPANY
681 FIFTH AVENUE

PREFACE

These letters were actually written at the times indicated by the wife of an American officer temporarily attached to the State Department as an Attaché to our Embassy at Petrograd.

They begin with the arrival in Russia and extend to the rather dramatic escape from that unfortunate and unpleasant sadly upset country, when all foreigners were seeking a safer place, except those Germans who appeared to be under the protection of the ones who are generally called Bolsheviks but who may more properly be termed Anarchists. The period they cover is one of great interest to poor Russia and consequently to the whole world, of which Russia as she was, formed such a large percentage in area and population. Much of political significance has necessarily been omitted from the original letters, and more from the copies that were retained and have been used in this volume, but the final proof represents the observations of one with exceptional opportunities to learn at the time what was really going on. The letters are not biased by any ulterior motives and only show what an observer knew would be of interest to intimate relatives and friends in the United States. May these letters now serve to interest and enlighten those others who would know what has not before been published!

P. S. C.

Chapter I
THE SIBERIAN RAILWAY

On the Siberian Railway,
Saturday,
April 28, 1917.

My dear—

At last we are in the sleeping car that is supposed to take us to Petrograd and we are away from Harbin.[1] I use the word "supposed" after some thought, for while I believe we will reach Petrograd in this car, there is no certainty about that.

Something is the matter in Russia! Of course we have read of the Russian Revolution, but we have not read of the things which make us wonder. While in Pekin [sic][2] Walter was advised by those who have made this trip to wear his uniform after leaving the region of Japanese influence. Yesterday morning, in the sleeper from Mukden,[3] he put it on, but while it is a new uniform it does not seem popular with the Russian soldiers. Moreover, there are some Russian generals and officers of less rank on this train who are not treated with courtesy by the soldiers. There is a look on the faces of the soldiers that almost frightens me at times, while again they seem to be well-disposed grown-up children. At Harbin yesterday the "heavy mental atmosphere" was apparent. It is becoming heavier!

I was worn out when we finally got to our berths last night at Harbin. It was most difficult to get our baggage attended to and it annoyed me to have two of our trunks broken by the surly porters we eventually succeeded in getting to handle them.

This morning, with the train in rapid motion, a gorgeous sunshine, snow on the nearby mountains, snow and ice in the streams, a wonderful landscape and something to eat, I feel more refreshed, but cannot convince myself, when the train stops at a station, that all is well in Russia.

---

[1] Harbin is located in northern China and was inhabited by many Russians in the late nineteenth century during the construction of the Trans-Siberian Railway. It was a major Russian refugee center during the Civil War and after. The war on the Western Front made it necessary for the Crosleys to travel to Petrograd through Siberia.

[2] Peking, China, now known as Beijing. In this period, Japan's empire was on the rise and it had already taken parts of China, as well as German territory in the region.

[3] Mukden, China, now known as Shenyang.

April 29th.

Having read the last line I wrote yesterday I repeat it!

Last evening we stopped at Manchuria, on the frontier of real Russian territory, where one must pass the Chinese and the Russian Customs officials. We had anticipated annoyance there, in view of all we had heard, and were armed with many official papers written in both languages, to lessen our troubles. All trunks were removed from the baggage car and taken into the station, where there was a great confusion. There was much conversation and finally a telegram from Petrograd was found by a Russian official directing that our trunks be allowed to accompany us to Petrograd without annoyance.

Walter had telegraphed from Pekin requesting such an arrangement because, owing to limited transportation facilities, a very small amount of baggage only is allowed on this train. The officials very gravely removed all the ropes from our trunks and then replaced them, *without opening the trunks*. It was evident at Manchuria that officials, *officers* and orders did not inspire respect. (Rubles were more potent!)

After our baggage troubles were completed we returned to our car to hear more unpleasantness; a Russian Priest who was returning to Russia from the United States had brought some condensed milk with him for use on the train; it was taken away from him by the "inspectors"; it was quite dark in our car and we learned that the dynamo was permanently disabled; very poor candle light is all we may expect now until we reach Petrograd; and this on the celebrated Trans-Siberian Express, in a "Wagon-Lit"! Something is certainly wrong in Russia.

We are fortunate in having as fellow passengers (not in our car, unfortunately), Mr. and Mrs. Corse[4] and Miss Potter, Americans who have lived many years in Russia and who are now returning from a visit in the United States to Petrograd. They all speak Russian and we manage to go to the dining car when they do, which makes it easier for us to order what we want, for the waiters speak only Russian. The compartment next to ours is occupied by an attractive Japanese couple, but the car itself is not clean; neither is the dining car nor are the waiters; the food will keep starvation away but it is far from being appetizing.

We were soundly asleep last night when there came a great hammering at our door. In our dubious frame of mind we wondered—but it was only because we were coming to a bridge and it was necessary that our door be open in order that the soldiers could see we did not throw bombs out of the window to damage the bridge. It is not pleasant to lie in one's berth and know that soldiers, concerning whose behavior there is good reason to have doubts, are looking at one, but we became quite accustomed to the sensation as there are many bridges!

---

[4] Frederick M. Corse (1872–1928) was the head of the Russian branch of the New York Life Insurance Company. His understanding of Russian politics and economics made him a valuable asset as an advisor to the US ambassador in Russia, David Francis.

April 30th.

Seemingly it will not be worthwhile to mail this letter while en route. We are told mails are unreliable; we believe it. I now expect to add to this letter as opportunity offers and mail it when there is a possibility it will reach you.

The weather and the landscape remain impressively beautiful; this morning we passed Lake Baikal and began to realize the engineering difficulties that had been overcome in building this road. We crossed more bridges and were guarded as before. There is an interesting mixture of races and nationalities on board this train. At a table of four in the dining car I observed a well maintained conversation being carried on in three languages.

Our train stopped nearly two hours at Irkutsk and we would have welcomed an opportunity for exercise and sight-seeing, but, owing to the now very evident disorganization we realize that the railroad officials do not know when the train may proceed, so we may not know either. No one wandered far from his own car; it would have been a real calamity to get left behind.

We have seen many red banners and have heard groups of Russians singing the Marseillaise. There are many revolutionary placards which we cannot read but which astonish our American friends who translate them for us. They find difficulty in realizing that this is Russia; they note the great changes that are not evident to us.

When we left Irkutsk a great many soldiers tried to board our train but the train porters were expecting the effort and managed to close and lock the doors in time to prevent many soldiers from entering the cars; the car steps are crowded with them and why they do not freeze and fall off I cannot imagine; I can see that some of them are asleep and the train is certainly not steady! I am obliged to pity them but the lack of organization, discipline, law and order is very apparent. "Free Russia" as translated for us from the many posters is not entirely free for us; we are practically prisoners in our car and there is ample evidence that "freedom" means more to these people than we understand the word to mean; it also means more for them than they intend it shall mean for us, which is annoying!

Walter did not wear his uniform today and he will keep it out of sight for the present. It is evident that the uniform of an officer is regarded with—suspicion, shall I say, by "free Russian soldiers," another frequent quotation from the posters that are growing more frequent. Something certainly is the matter with the Russian Army!

Thursday, May first.

The wonderful weather we have been having has failed us and changed for the worse; so has the Russian political situation as viewed from a "Wagon Lit" window. Soldiers have now forced their way into the train in spite of the verbal protests of the Russian Army officers and the train officials, sometimes breaking car fittings to accomplish their purpose. During the night we were awakened each time the train stopped by soldiers attempting to force an entrance into our car. It seems they do not break doors and windows in this car because they have been taught that the "Wagon Lits" are foreign property and there is still left a small amount of respect for foreigners and foreign property; our American friends tell us that the Russian officers use as an argument with the soldiers when trying to influence them to let the train alone "what will the foreigners think of free Russia?"

Soldiers have practically filled all cars but ours on the train and it is only a question of time when the desire to ride free will overcome the respect for foreign property. It is now very difficult to get to the dining car because one must climb over soldiers in all vestibules and corridors. Poor food, foul air, dirt, discomfort and cold are beginning to affect me unpleasantly and I am not well. Fortunately I have some simple remedies in my hand bag, but I am assured that the Russian Grippe germ will not yield to simple remedies! I must not become really ill, for I am obliged to go on—there is no place to stop. Today we saw evidences on the part of some soldiers to observe law and order and to prevent "joy riding" on this train by those without railroad tickets. The effort was a mild one and did not have an appreciable effect.

May third.

I have had two wretched days. I can no longer eat the food in the dining car. Our American friends have been lovely to me and they are able to purchase some few things to eat when the train stops. Our Japanese neighbors have given me a basket of fruit they brought from Japan and we brought with us such provisions as could be safely carried, so I will not really suffer. Our dear old porter does his best to make me comfortable.

We have passed many forest fires; our Russian fellow-passengers tell us the fires are started by the soldiers and peasants simply to destroy. "Freedom" looks more and more like "License" and this belief is forced upon us by the increasing number of soldiers taking free rides with us; the train officials can do nothing with the soldiers; the Russian officers have ceased trying.

May fourth.

I am feeling better, thanks to kind attention and some rest, but the weather and the soldiers are growing worse! We enjoyed our first sight of the "white nights" last night. It was quite light at ten o'clock and the sun did not set until after eight.

The soldiers are now a great annoyance; they have invaded our sleeping car and some came into the diner. One in our car interests me much; he has a childlike face, a child's complexion, eyes like a baby, yet is a giant in strength and has a bushy red beard; his hair is also red and long; I cannot believe *he* is bad, yet the horrible tales we are hearing of brutality practiced by his fellow-kind makes one think! It is easy to believe that some of the free-riding soldiers are not good; their faces are very interesting. "My soldier" has been helping keep other soldiers out of our car. He is very grateful for some food and cigarettes Walter gave him; we think we will keep him as a volunteer guard; it seems he wishes to go to Petrograd but has no real reason for going; he simply has never been there and now that he is free he may go without paying. We do not leave the car when the train stops, because it is no longer safe; we would return to find our compartment filled with soldiers; crowds of soldiers are at all stations trying to crowd into the train.

May fifth.
This has been an exciting day. I am feeling much better but have an annoying sore throat. We arrived at Vologda at one o'clock in the afternoon; it is a junction for Moscow and Archangel;[5] the station was "jammed" with soldiers, also with peasants of both sexes and all ages. Here we saw the first members of the "White Guard,"[6] of which we have been hearing rumors for several days. Some fine looking Russians, armed and wearing a white band on one arm, boarded the train and removed, by persuasion and force, every soldier except one! That one was "my soldier" who was advised by Walter (he made signs—for our study of the Russian language has not yet made us conversationalists in that tongue) to go in the lavatory and lock the door; his equipment was hidden under the wood in the wood bin and the White Guard did not find him; he was in there some time and you should have seen him when he came out, after the train had left Vologda! His face shone, his hair and beard were neatly combed, he had cleaned his uniform, and he was as pleased and happy as any child you ever saw! I believe I would like to annex him, he seems so dependable in this Russia we now know is so badly upset.

We are due in Petrograd at ten o'clock tonight but will not arrive at that hour; no one in the train can tell us when we *will* arrive. The railroad service is sadly demoralized and even from the car window we can see that other industries are in a similar condition. It is now nine o'clock in the evening and I am writing by the daylight that enters the compartment window. We find the white nights a very great comfort when the dynamo furnishes no light in the car.

---

[5] Archangel is an important port city in the north. In both world wars, it served as a point of entry for aid from Russia's allies.

[6] The White Guard refers to the anti-Bolshevik forces that fought against the new "Red" regime in the Civil War of 1918–21.

When you receive this you will know we did reach Petrograd. We must not undress for we *might* arrive while asleep and I wish to escape as soon as possible. Oh! How I will welcome unlimited fresh water and a tub! Please give our love to —— and —— and ——. I will write to you again when I am temporarily settled and partly comfortable.

Affectionately yours,

Chapter II
PETROGRAD

Hotel d'Europe,[1]
Petrograd,
May 9, 1917.

My very dear—

We are here, and a busy three days I have had. Our train reached Petrograd after five a.m. on the sixth, but we were called at two in the morning. The gray dawn was not cheerful nor were the countenances of those who had waited all night at the very dingy station for their friends who were expected to arrive on our train. We lost "the soldier" before the train stopped. Captain McCully, U.S.N.,[2] met us and we drove to this hotel where he had been able, fortunately for us, to engage a small room; all Petrograd is crowded and it will not be easy for us to find a place to live. We parted from our agreeable fellow passengers with mutual promises to meet again soon; on the way to the hotel our izvozchik[3] (really the driver but now generally used to indicate the whole conveyance) proudly pointed out to us many bullet marks on buildings and bullet holes in windows. We learned that we had just missed a revolution against the Provisional Government,[4] which had been quickly suppressed. We also learned that all is not well in Russia; that a great unrest prevails, and, what is most alarming, that the continuance of Russia in the war is problematical! Walter first heard that we had entered the war while we were at Mukden and he has been very eager to arrive here and do his part and see some real fighting with the Russian Fleet; it now appears that the Russian Fleet will do no more fighting and that the Russian Army has begun to disintegrate.

---

[1] Opened in 1875, the Hotel Europe was the oldest and premier hotel in Petrograd. It still operates today.

[2] Newton A. McCully (1867–1951) was an American vice admiral and naval attaché at the American embassy in Petrograd from 1914–17. He was also commander of the American naval forces in northern Russian waters from 1918–19.

[3] *Izvozchik* means cab, or cabbie.

[4] The Provisional Government was formed after the abdication of Nicholas II in February (March) 1917. It consisted mostly of Duma members and other officials from the more liberal and moderate parties.

We have already met many people from many countries and, as with the Russian language, have learned a great deal at the beginning of our stay in Petrograd of what has happened in Russia and what may be expected in the near future. Much that we have learned does not correspond with what we have had read to us in the public press while en route and what we read in the newspapers we found waiting for us here.

I cannot tell you how comfortable the bed in the hotel is after eleven days on the train! I *can* tell you that the outlook for proper food to eat is not encouraging. While there is a certain amount of provisions to be had, the menu is neither appetizing nor satisfying. Immediately after a very expensive dinner at this hotel we both longed for something to eat!

Everyone has been most agreeable to us; we attended a reception at the Embassy the night of our arrival, meeting all of the Embassy Staff and many resident Americans. Captain McCully, U.S.N., gave a tea, with dancing, in his apartment, where we met many of his charming Russian friends and the other Allied Attaches and their families.

Walter has taken over his new duties and has been busy making his official calls. We have both been seeking an apartment in which to live; we had arranged to take the one Captain McCully has been occupying when a cable from Washington changed his plans and ours. We have looked at many apartments for we cannot continue to live at this hotel in any comfort.

Once again it is proven that this is a small world; a friend we knew in Turkey has just called; Walter recognized in the American occupant of an apartment at which we looked a gentleman he had recently met in Philadelphia. I have known the American Consul here for many years; he comes from my "home town" and we have many friends in common. So you see we are not "strangers in a strange land" at all, which helps wonderfully in overcoming the many difficulties we will encounter. One of those difficulties is the language; I have never been anywhere and found the language of the country such a necessity. I am studying hard but one does not make rapid progress at first in an entirely new tongue, and while I know a little of several languages, that knowledge does not help me with Russian! It is entirely a question of study and memory. We have a waiter for our room at the hotel who speaks German; the use of that language is forbidden and some have been fined for using it; we whisper our wants in German!

Consul Winship[5] took us to the opera, where he has a box. The Russian opera is wonderful and I am going to love it. The Opera House is large and is very dingy on the outside but, in spite of the many changes the Revolution has brought about, inside it is still beautiful. The handsome Imperial blue drop curtain has been replaced by an odd red-and-gold one; the Imperial Eagle was on the blue one. The Crown and Eagle

---

[5] North Winship (1885–1968), from Macon, GA, served as the American consul in Petrograd and later as the US minister to South Africa.

above the Czar's box have been covered with cloth. All over Petrograd similar symbols on buildings, fences, bridges, monuments, etc., have been removed or defaced. The white and gold finish of the Opera House, with "Russian blue" draperies, and the comfortable salon chairs for seats, still show the grandeur of the place, but we are told it is not cared for as formerly and already shows the effect of neglect.

The contrast between the former brilliant audience and the present somber one is brought to our attention by those who have lived a long while in Russia. Now, one sees soldiers, sailors and peasants occupying the Royal Box and there is none of the former brilliancy of smart gowns and gorgeous uniforms. While we were at the Opera a voice from the highest gallery demanded the Marseillaise; the orchestra played it and everyone stood; it would have been unsafe to remain seated. I saw one woman who did remain, but a rough looking man sprang toward her with menacing gesture and loud voice; she rose sulkily, and when the man turned away she slowly slid into her chair, then quickly stood again.

We hear many conflicting reports of what has happened and what may be expected to happen. I am meeting the people, making notes, and I promise you soon some news, which of course must pass the censor, but may differ from what you have read in the newspapers. Mail is uncertain and unsafe; it partakes of the general demoralization that becomes more evident each day. Food is scarce and is certain to become more so; fuel, (wood, there is no coal) is *most* difficult to obtain though there are miles of it a few versts[6] outside of Petrograd, but it cannot be transported. Fortunately it is growing warmer but I have shivered much since my arrival.

Our best love to all and please do not stop writing; we will not receive all our mail but we want all we can get.

Always affectionately yours,

Hotel d'Europe,
Petrograd,
May 15, 1917.

My very dear—

This will doubtless be a long letter, for I continue to learn facts, as well as the Russian language!

In our tiresome hunt for an apartment I have met many very interesting and very well informed people and I have made many notes. There are but few "houses" in Petrograd, only palaces and apartments. We find we can get one of several palaces, but the inevitable grave difficulty of maintaining one or even heating it, not to mention the responsibilities of its care and the care of what it contains, decided us against taking one. We have taken an unsatisfactory apartment on Kirochnaya, num-

---

[6] A verst is roughly equivalent to two-thirds of a mile.

ber eight, but it will only be temporary, for the Americans who occupy it and who are leaving immediately expect to return in about three months. That will give us time to find what we want if there will be such available.

It would amuse you to hear the remarkable and varied stories concerning the March Revolution, when the Czar was deposed. One must listen to all of them and form an idea from the reliability of the informant. You will appreciate this when I tell you that I have been informed by one who was in an official position sufficiently important to have enabled him to know, that only one hundred and sixty people were killed in Petrograd in March! Another reliable eyewitness said he saw that many dead at one corner and he estimated the total dead in three days, from what he saw himself, at five thousand! I have met some who were in this hotel at the time and who have told me of the numerous raids and searches here. The searches were very complete and no person nor thing was exempt. Money and jewelry were taken, as well as anything else that appealed to the fancy of the raiders who were quite strong on intimidation, and who were well armed to give weight to their threats. It is believed that many of the released criminals put on officers' and soldiers' uniforms and carried on these raids, but of course they were not all made by such men. The period was one of wild scenes of terror; palaces and apartments were searched as well as hotels. The apartment we are to occupy was searched thirteen times in three days.

Of course the secret police came in for the worst hatred, for much we have read of that wonderful organization was true enough to have brought down the hatred of all classes upon the heads of its members. They were hunted through the streets and homes and killed instantly when found. Police stations were burned with the intention of destroying the police records, but, as an example of the work ahead of someone in "Reconstructed Russia," at the same time thousands of the land records were burned and there will be no official title to most of the estates!

Now one sees hundreds of groups on the street corners being addressed by "soap box orators" in impassioned speech, much of which savors of anarchy and none of which looks to a formation of law and order or a return to an organized condition. "What good are aristocrats? They have never done anything in their lives!" "Down with capital!" are frequent cries of these street orators, but when questioned as to what is *an aristocrat* they do not know, but agree that anyone who is educated and "groomed" is in that class. When asked how a factory can run without capital they assert they will run it, but they do not know from what land the raw material is obtained nor what it costs. It is very noticeable that Russians are fluent public speakers, and that a great many of the groups originally being addressed by one person soon dissolve into howling mobs in which each member believes himself to be the only statesman present.

I promised to give you a bit of history of events, but there is so much of it I find it difficult to know what to leave out! It is certain that the Germans, in their fiendish cleverness, had able assistants in Russia, and even in high places in this Capital. It is also *certain* there were patriotic Russians in the Duma[7] and elsewhere who sought to overcome this traitorous influence. Probably the first open effort in the Duma to do this began in December, 1916, when some of these patriots made eloquent speeches, arguing for the organization that would make Russia invincible and calling attention to the faults of the existing Government. Thus began a visible conflict between the Duma and the Government, though of course individuals had seen and tried to remedy the defects. The dismissal of Mr. Sturmer[8] by the Czar on November 23, 1916, and the appointment of Mr. Trepov,[9] as President of the Council of Ministers, was doubtless a result of the agitation then under way.

The assassination of Rasputin[10] on December 30, 1916, brought about a climax in government affairs, for this strange man, with unusual psychical and mental powers—doubtless a mesmerist—was certainly a power in Russia owing to the large following he had of religious fanatics and political sycophants. He wielded strong influences and when he was removed chaos resulted in certain circles. At the same time charges of corruption against Government Ministers began to be made openly—and also that some Russians in high places were in direct communication with the Germans, making preparations for a separate peace.

All of this precipitated a great unrest and probably brought about the Revolution at the time it actually occurred, or made possible the spreading of the bread riots into a revolution. I have been assured that a revolution had been "in the making" for some months, by the master minds of patriotic Russians, but that it was to be postponed until our German enemies were defeated. Undoubtedly the Germans saw their chance in all this turmoil and were instrumental in hastening the chaos. Yet these same Germans now insinuated that *some of our Allies* did that very thing! Clever—are they not!

---

[7] In 1905, after ten months of revolution and public disturbances, Nicholas II created the Duma—from the Russian word *dumat'* (to think)—a pseudo-Parliament that looked promising on paper but would never be allowed to function as a truly representative body. For example, when the first two Dumas became too critical of the government, Nicholas II simply dissolved them.

[8] Boris Stürmer (1848–1917) served as chairman of the Council of Ministers from January to November 1916. He was arrested and imprisoned in the Peter Paul Fortress after the February Revolution by the Provisional Government. He died in prison of kidney failure.

[9] Alexander Trepov (1868–1928) succeeded Stürmer as chairman of the Council of Ministers, November–December 1916.

[10] Grigory Rasputin (1872–1916) was the peasant "holy man" who became very close to the Romanov royal family because of his ability to calm and slow the bleeding of the heir to the throne, Aleksei, who suffered from hemophilia. As a consequence, Nicholas II and Alexandra became dependent on Rasputin and their trust in him soon extended to other areas, including political matters. This, combined with his influence over and seduction of many of the noble wives of the capital, made him much reviled, and resulted in his murder by a group of noblemen in December 1916.

From all I can learn, the financial condition of Russia cannot be considered as satisfactory. Of course the war has made great drains on the Treasury, and while Russian individuals have many rubles in the banks and secreted, they cannot buy much with a ruble. This causes dissatisfaction, and such steps as the Government seems to have taken to improve matters probably cause more. For example, the peasant must sell his wheat, butter, eggs, etc., at a price set by the Government. He must buy his boots at a price set by the man who has boots to sell. There are many peasants, hence much complaining.

One of the most impressive things here is the safety in which one may walk the streets at night. We do a great deal of walking, there being no other form of exercise available, and because we can best learn the city (and what is going on) that way.

Here is a Nation without a flag; a Capital with no police force; one sees occasionally a man with a rifle, wearing a white band on his arm, standing or sitting at a street corner. No other protection is in evidence, yet I have not heard of any violence or theft since our arrival! We hear of much that took place during and immediately after the March Revolution. It will be simply wonderful if matters continue this way, but I do not see how they can. As soon as the lawless and the released criminals learn how easy it is to "rob and run away" the present security will end, but up to date it can only be described as marvelous. The absence of drunkenness is likewise very noticeable. Everyone familiar with Russia tells us what a curse vodka (very cheap) and its effects were. To note that we have not seen a drunken man in our ten days here indicates what a change has been brought about.

This letter is long enough! I will try to write you a weekly letter so you may know just what we are doing. I will write you more about the Revolution of March next week.

With all love,
Your—

Kirochnaya, Vosyem,
Petrograd,
May 22, 1917.

Well—My dear—

A very busy week has passed and it is fortunate for my promise to you that I have taken notes, as I could never remember all that takes place any more than I can remember all the Russian I hear.

We are in our temporary apartment; moved in the rain just after I wrote you last week. The rain stopped after we had moved and we have had fine weather generally, though it snowed the day before yesterday. What would you think if it snowed nearly all day in Washington on May 20th?

We have had a luncheon at the handsome apartment of Consul Winship, a dinner with our American friends of the Siberian Railway trip who live in the most modern apartment in the city, which is situated across the Neva, a dinner with our Counselor, Mr. Butler Wright,[11] and his wife, have been to the ballet with Ambassador Francis[12] and to a luncheon given for us at the Restaurant Donon, so you see we are having a few diversions.

The Russian Ballet! The Russian Ballet dancers! No—they are butterflies! Each representation is a pantomime of an interesting fairy or other story and I shall never tire of seeing them. Our more critical friends say that even the stage suffers on account of the revolution and that mistakes are made for which a punishment would have been awarded "before the revolution," but it seems perfection to me. To this ballet school also very small girls of excellent families are sent; many stars are developed to shine brilliantly; the training of the artists does not cease until they are retired for age. It will be a calamity indeed if this Russian art becomes a thing of the past, for nothing more beautiful and graceful can take its place.

I have taken up active work, sewing, here in the American Lazaret.[13] The Americans of Petrograd started this hospital for Russian soldiers where they have all worked and spent money to a very great advantage indeed. By their efforts they have shown many a wounded Russian soldier what comfort really is, and have taught them trades wherewith they may, though crippled, earn a livelihood. When the soldiers go to their homes after being discharged from the American Lazaret each one carries with him a bag of clothes and other useful articles the amount of which depends upon the size of his family. Touching, appreciative letters have been received at the Lazaret, written by these men from their homes, and Miss Potter has translated many, having them printed in a pamphlet. Certainly this group of American patriots deserves credit it will never receive for the "American Propaganda" it has spread, the good effect of which cannot be denied. I am glad to add my mite to the great work.

The soldiers and sailors in and near the Black Sea have remained in a state of discipline far in advance of any others of which I can learn, except the ever faithful Cossacks. On Saturday last a large Committee from Sevastopol, made up of sailors from the Russian Black Sea Fleet and of soldiers from the Sevastopol Garrison arrived in Petrograd and held an open meeting to which all were invited, with patriotic

---

[11] Joshua Butler Wright (1877–1939) was counselor to the American embassy in Petrograd, 1916–18, and left one of the only day-to-day accounts by an American of the revolution as it unfolded. His diaries and letters of that period have been published under the title *Witness to Revolution: The Russian Revolution Diary and Letters of J. Butler Wright*.

[12] David R. Francis (1850–1927) was ambassador to Russia in 1916–21 and later published a book about his experiences as a witness to the Russian Revolution. See David R. Francis, *Russia from the American Embassy*, ed. Vladimir V. Noskov (Bloomington, IN: Slavica, 2019).

[13] The American Lazaret was a hospital for Russian soldiers created by a group of Americans living in Petrograd.

intent. Enthusiastic speeches were made by members of the Committee urging the necessity of remaining in the war. Evidently this group has also decided that "all is not well in Russia"! Our Ambassador made a fine speech which was most excellently interpreted by a Russian Naval Officer and which was received with much cheering by the audience, but from what I have seen I suspect that a Russian audience is always ready to cheer the latest speaker.

There has been an arrangement by which those attached to foreign Embassies and Legations could purchase flour, butter, eggs and a small amount of wood from the Russian Government. We have not been able to profit by that arrangement and it appears it may, like other conveniences, quite disappear. The struggle for food and fuel has begun in earnest. It is lucky, first, that summer will soon be here, and second, that we brought considerable foodstuff with us.

The general unrest has begun to crystallize in a menacing series of strikes. Managers of factories are being forced, at the muzzles of many pistols and rifles, to increase wages to a degree that can only result in closing the factories, and this at a time when the output of every factory is needed more than ever before, and the wages received absolutely essential to maintain life. Also, at a time when raw materials, in some cases, cost *one thousand times* what they formerly cost! Imagine prohibitive wages under those conditions! Men in charge of large business offices in Petrograd and Moscow are being similarly forced to increase salaries beyond all possibility of remaining in business. Probably geese that lay golden eggs have never before been murdered on such a large scale, and the final result is inevitable; every industry so attacked must fail; the number attacked is increasing daily.

We are very cheerful for it would be useless to be otherwise, but one can't help seeing what is so evident as the ultimate ruin of Russia. It is all so interesting to me as I get it day by day from those I meet who have helped to make the history and from those who saw it being made. I only wish I could give you all I receive but time and space will not permit. As a matter of news, I can tell you that Finland is showing signs of "secession"; I am not in a position to advise you as to the right or the wrong of this, but I believe Russia will lose that interesting part of her former Empire. (There are other parts of Russia from which signs of a similar uneasiness come, and all is *less* well in Russia.)

We walk about the streets at night, sometimes with an interpreter, viewing the bread and other food lines. Even now, when it is cold after the sun gets low, long lines of men, women and children sleep all night on the pavements in front of provision shops waiting for them to open in the morning. Some of these lines extend for several blocks. These "bread lines" and the riots they caused really started the revolution prematurely in March. Working people from the suburbs whose factories had closed swarmed into Petrograd, where police and Cossacks patrolled and threatened the mob. At the same time regiments of soldiers were kept ready to move from their barracks. Immediately before the final crash, shops were closed and street cars stopped running. This latter measure is a common one in Petrograd and is put into effect, apparently, for two purposes—to prevent the transportation of the mob and to preserve the cars! There was a clash between the mob and the police (who were reinforced by Cossacks) on March 10th, but, though many shots were fired, probably few were killed or wounded and the mob began to believe that the soldiers would not handle it as severely as they had in former times.

The next day, Sunday, March 11th, more firing took place and it seems that more than a hundred people were killed in different parts of the city, but by late that night, when many more of the troops had been called out, all seemed quiet and the law-abiding began to hope that the end had come.

The Nevsky Prospect has always been a gathering place for disorderly crowds and a large part of it was closed to traffic that night to prevent mobs gathering. But during the night the disorderly mobs had organized and the next day they appeared as real revolutionists, with objectives in view and a determination to capture Petrograd, which they proceeded to do, for during this day practically all the garrison of the city, about 25,000 men, went over to the revolutionists, though there was considerable fighting among the soldiers and many were killed, a large percentage of the dead being officers, some of whom committed suicide—most likely to avoid the decision then necessary as to whether or not they would join the Revolution.

Among the regiments which joined the people was the famous Guards Preobrazhensky Regiment,[14] the origin of which was the formation of the boyhood playmates of Peter the Great into a military body in imitation of their elders. When he became Czar he formed the regiment with his friends as the nucleus and it was considered a great honor to belong to it. That regiment had always been considered the *most* loyal to the Czar and when it "went over" the question of which side the soldiers would take was settled, so far as Petrograd was concerned.

It has always been difficult to learn the number of killed during the street fighting in Russia. The authorities have removed the dead to prevent facts from being known; the relatives of the dead remove and conceal them to avoid becoming implicated in the riots.

It is a matter of record and statement of eyewitnesses at this time that but few officers could be seen with the troops; possibly if they had been led by loyal officers the soldiers would have fired on the mob instead of joining it and the revolution would have failed, with many more dead. Many assert that the majority of the officers had agreed that they would join a revolutionary movement, but this one had come before the time set for it and that the officers did not know what to do.

---

[14] The Preobrazhensky Regiment refers to a special elite military unit first created by Peter the Great in the late seventeenth century.

It has been positively stated, and has appeared in the newspapers, that Mr. Rodzianko,[15] President of the Duma at the time of the revolution, telegraphed the situation to the Czar and to leading Generals of the Army, before the serious demonstrations began and during the earlier part of the real disorders, urging prompt measures to save the Empire, but without receiving any word from the Czar. Some believe the telegrams were withheld from His Majesty; others assert that he did not believe the danger, as reported, existed. The shooting increased with the success of the revolutionaries, though efforts were made by thinking members of the Duma to organize for law and order. Public buildings were seized, their guards being replaced by soldiers who had revolted. Prisons and jails were among the buildings taken and it was at this time the political, military and criminal prisoners were released in wholesale numbers. Many people were killed, officers who refused to give up their arms were murdered on the spot, the mob showing no mercy to anyone who failed to comply instantly with its demands. Red flags began to appear and all other flags to disappear, as well as all symbols representing the Empire.

At this time began what are said to have been the most gruesome and terrifying scenes of all; automobiles were seized, as well as motor trucks, and filled with armed men and machine guns; they went dashing about the city without apparent destination, but occasionally firing volleys at nothing in particular. Peaceful residents kept close in their homes and some have told me they were terrified enough.

By the end of the third day there was no organized resistance, all the troops still loyal apparently having left the city and the police being dead or in hiding; here and there a misguided patriot would alone oppose the mob, only to lose his life. It seems to have been a custom in Russia for anarchists to throw bombs from windows and, anyone wishing to shoot into a crowd, to do so from such a point of vantage. It is related that, during the days of fighting in March, all one had to do in order to commit suicide was to show himself at a window in the neighborhood where there was fighting; on both sides of the streets men with rifles were stationed, to shoot into the windows of the opposite side when a head appeared. At this time it was reported that loyal troops were on their way to Petrograd to suppress the revolution, and preparations were made by the revolutionists to meet them, but it is reported that, while there was some doubt as to the attitude the advancing troops would take, the majority of the revolutionists were firm in the belief that they would join in the revolution.

Now I have written enough for this week. I intend to continue my notes and write you just a little bit more of this history, with each letter I send you. We are expecting mail early next week and it will be most welcome.

Always affectionately yours,

---

[15] Mikhail Rodzianko (1850–1924) was chairman of the Fourth State Duma. He despised Rasputin and attempted to undermine his position with Nicholas II. He was a leading figure in the February Revolution that overthrew the tsar, but after the Bolshevik Revolution, he left Petrograd and eventually died abroad.

Kirochnaya, Vosyem,
Petrograd,
May 29, 1917.

My dear Son:

As you know, I am trying to write a series of letters and this will be one of them. I have arranged so you will receive all those I believe to be of interest to you, and will ask you to send this one to your brother, who will pass it along in accordance with the list I have furnished him. I simply cannot find the time to write to everyone as I would like, but our plan of forwarding these letters to other members of the family will serve excellently to give all news from us.

During the last week we have had generally fine weather, but have had to burn some of our precious wood in the large stove to enable us to keep warm enough. We build a fire of wood, wait till the smoke and fumes get out of it, then close the stove *tight* on the bright red coals. An efficient stove stays warm a long time but I am heartily glad that warmer weather will soon be with us. We are still unable to obtain flour, sugar and wood; the general food situation grows worse daily. A member of the Embassy staff called a few days ago and brought me a very handsome present—a loaf of *white* bread!!

We have been to three dinner parties, a luncheon and some teas this week, so we are not always hungry! Probably owing to the quality of what one gets to eat it doesn't satisfy for long. After a meal, of course, one is not hungry, but very soon afterward another meal would be acceptable. As you are familiar with our modest appetites you will understand what I mean.

Immediately after our arrival in Petrograd, at the reception given by Captain McCully, we met, among others, Prince and Princess Maksutov, a truly charming couple. We have been to their house and they have been here; all four agree that we must be good friends, and I hope we will find others so attractive and friendly.

I have been inspecting the provision shops with Mrs. Gaylord,[16] an American who has been here for nearly twenty years with her husband and who kindly offered to help me learn the shops. We found a small amount of oatmeal and immediately bought it; a real treasure! My list of acquaintances grows and I have met more interesting and attractive Russians. In spite of the conditions I am going to like Russia and the Russians. I have continued work in the Lazaret; our sewing days there furnish opportunities for the American women to meet, and as the most of them have been several years in Russia, I learn much of value and interest from them.

One of the sad but sure signs of a decaying Russia is the lack of repair one sees on every hand; this was first and most noticeable on the Siberian Railroad, before we reached Petrograd, but here it is true of streets, vehicles, buildings, *everything*.

---

[16] Mrs. Gaylord was the wife of Franklin Gaylord (1856–1943), who spent eighteen years in Russia helping to establish *Mayak* (Lighthouse), an affiliate of the Young Men's Christian Association.

In my last letter I got as far as Monday, March 12, when, so far as Petrograd was concerned, the revolution was a success and everyone was wondering what the Army would do. Some troops began to arrive from out of town but they were met at the railroad stations by committees of the revolutionists and were quickly won over.

Wholesale arrests were now the order of the day and it seems that opportunity was taken to get revenge for personal wrongs, or fancied wrongs—hatreds; the arrests included all the Ministers, such of the police as were not killed as soon as located, also many minor officers and officials. To indicate the temper of the mob, it was this day the Hotel Astoria, the newest and most modern hotel in the city, which had been commandeered under the old regime for officers of the Army and Navy, was attacked and considerably injured. The mob believed shots had been fired from its windows so they charged and "captured" it, firing many shots and killing a few people. They searched it thoroughly and arrested many on suspicion. Searches and arrests continued throughout the city and if a suspect resisted he was immediately killed.

The next day was a continuation of what had gone before but efforts were made to establish some sort of order. News from other parts of Russia indicated they were following Petrograd's lead and success. Red flags multiplied and flags or other emblems of the old regime disappeared with absolute completeness. A semblance of organization and an attempt to form a government was started. The hunt for the police continued, though the real power of that once powerful organization was destroyed in one day.

Many of the criminals who had been released were again arrested and confined; in general, a serious effort was made to control the lawless and that effort being continued is responsible for the security we now feel in walking where we will at night. Great credit is due those whose self-restraint led them to destroy stores of wine and liquor instead of drinking it, and this example by itself shows that the March Revolution was a serious one, in which those taking part knew, to be successful, they must avoid drunkenness; their manifest desire to make matters better was evident. That a smooth working machine for good government has not yet begun to work is not remarkable; what real government was ever established in three months?

In all my inquiries I have not, until this week, learned from what I consider a reliable source just what happened when the Czar abdicated, though many accounts were printed at the time. I believe I can tell you now for I have it from a very intelligent intimate relative of Mr. Guchkov[17] who, with a member of the Duma, Mr. Shulgine,[18] went from Petrograd to Pskov, to which place the Czar had proceeded

---

[17] A. I. Guchkov (1862–1936) was a Duma member sent as a representative of the Provisional Government to demand the abdication of Nicholas II. He served as minister of war for a short period in the new Provisional Government; when he resigned, he was succeeded by Kerensky.

[18] Vasily Shulgin (1878–1976) was sent as a representative of the Provisional Government to demand the abdication of Nicholas II in February 1917.

from Mogilev, Army Headquarters, when his train had been prevented by the revolutionists from going to Tsarskoe Selo or Petrograd.[19] These two carried with them a form of abdication which had been agreed upon in the Duma, it being the intention that the Czar should abdicate in favor of his young son, Alexis, but that the brother of the Czar, the Grand Duke Michael, would be made regent.

There was a short discussion in the Czar's train, Mr. Guchkov stating the requirements to the Czar who replied that, owing to the ill health of his son (the boy was hemophiliac), he preferred to abdicate in favor of the Grand Duke Michael. The representatives of the Duma, after a short consultation, agreed to this and the Czar immediately signed the abdication, the night of March fifteenth. Those who were present at the interview seemed to have been much impressed by the calmness of the whole affair; there seems to have been no visible excitement on the part of anyone present!

In the meantime a temporary government had been formed in Petrograd and the former Czar returned to Army Headquarters where it is reported he was not received in even a friendly manner by those who had been his intimates; it was there, at Mogilev, that he was arrested on March 21st by a Committee of the Duma, accompanied by the new Military Governor of Petrograd, who went to Mogilev for the purpose. His wife, the unfortunate ex-Czarina, with all her children, was arrested the same day at Tsarskoe Selo by another committee from Petrograd; the ex-Czar joined them the next day and the entire family has been kept there under guard at their palace since then. Many of the revolutionists seem to enjoy calling the former Czar "Colonel Romanov"; one sees it in the newspapers rather frequently. I cannot but feel, if my judgment of Russian character is even partly correct, that the ex-Royal Family will yet suffer more than they have suffered. In this Russia as I see it, nothing is impossible. There is a feeling against that family, expressed not openly but by insinuation, which leads me to believe they are in greater danger than ever before; and not only that family, but others who have been occupying high places in Russia.[20]

Please do not decide I am a pessimist; I am anything but that; however, I see and learn so much that convinces me of the *unreliability*, to put it mildly, of the Russian masses. I am told of the disorders and of the murder of officers all along the Russian fronts; of the murder of officers in the Black Sea Fleet; of the most unusual and unnecessary steps taken by the revolutionists outside of Petrograd to cause suffering; of the excesses at Kronstadt;[21] of the failure of well-meaning Russian politicians now in the

---

[19] Tsarskoe Selo was an imperial palace south of the city.

[20] Nicholas II, his family, and his servants were executed in the summer of 1918 at the hands of the new Bolshevik government.

[21] Founded by Peter the Great on Kotlin Island, Kronstadt served as a military base and training center, about twenty miles to the west of Petrograd at the approach to the Gulf of Finland.

Government to control the vindictive lower classes, and I cannot see anything bright in Russia's future at present.

Of course I do not talk like this to my Russian friends, for I believe I already have several friends among those I have met several times. I try to cheer them and I succeed, but Oh! again how glad I am that I am an American! It is certain that there has been a change for the worse in the three weeks we have been here. If we can see it in three weeks it must be very evident. I again wonder if the Germans are not having a great deal to say in all this and I am beginning to feel sure that they are; it is all so like what they would wish to happen to Russia!

It is late, and one does not get a normal amount of sleep with "white nights" and entertaining friends and acquaintances all trying to prevent it! I have been learning all I can of the present government here and next week I will try to tell about it. Keep well, work hard, and believe in my great desire to see you.

A heart full of love from your father and Mother.

Kirochnaya, 8,
Petrograd,
June 5, 1917.

My other dear Son:

My last letter went to your brother but of course you will have seen that as well as my former letters before you receive this. Real correspondence is out of the question for we estimate that about three months will be required to receive an answer to a letter written from either end of the line. Even that period is uncertain, so do not be surprised if you fail to receive prompt answers to questions!

We are fully enjoying the warmer fine weather which reduces the fuel question to that necessary for cooking. Our need became so great we had to borrow wood from the Dvornik—(a sort of janitor who carries wood from the basement to one's apartment). Your father, after continued effort, managed to procure about two cords of wood which, without decrease by theft, will last us a month.

There is a remarkable system of what is called in the Far East "cumshaw" and in the United States sometimes called "graft," we have discovered in connection with the wood proposition! One buys wood by the sahjen, about two-thirds of a cord; each sahjen contains ten visiyankas; one pays for a sahjen and *nine* visiyankas are delivered; of these nine the Dvornik gets one (plus a wage from the owner of the house plus a monthly money gift from the occupant of the apartment). The remaining eight visiyankas shrink somewhat when other occupants of apartments find it necessary to borrow, as we did! There is a system of wood tickets supposed to protect the owner of the wood from such losses, but in this case protection does not protect.

We have again been to dinners and luncheons and teas, making new acquaintances and becoming better acquainted with those we have met before. It is perfectly legitimate to ask a hostess in Petrograd where she found any part of the dinner and what she had to pay for it!

Many Russian officers have called at your father's office with a request, in each case, that they be sent to the United States to join our Army or Navy. The number of these callers increases and not a day passes without one or more coming for such a request. It is difficult to convince them that our laws prevent what they desire, and while they cannot have their wish gratified one must be sorry for them. There is very little in sight for them in Russia; many of them come in disguise; they are in hiding because they were more or less prominent under the old regime and they would be killed or imprisoned if recognized now. Your father invites some of them to luncheon or dinner with us and they are sources of valuable information as well as interesting narrative. They *are* so confiding; they trust us absolutely and do not hesitate to tell anything they know! In addition, they are charming guests and we like some of them very much indeed.

It may be, as stated, that only fifteen per cent of the population of Russia is educated, but even if that is true my short experience here shows that percentage to be very *well* educated. It is not wonderful that the Russians are linguists; the deeper I get in the study of their own language, the more reason I see for their ease in mastering and using others!

Your father is obliged to have his office in our apartment and, to my great satisfaction he has obtained the services of a very attractive young lady as interpreter. Her father was a Colonel on the personal staff of the Czar and when the crash came he was arrested as a "suspect" and imprisoned for seven weeks in the Fortress of Peter and Paul.[22] The young daughter decided she must utilize her excellent education to help the family and I am very glad she is to come here.

The food problem becomes more difficult though the Government seems at times stronger and we hope that reconstruction has really begun. Occasionally one sees soldiers drilling in the streets and drill grounds, though the number is very small as compared with the number of soldiers in Petrograd; some are leaving from time to time, with more or less flourish ostensibly for "the front," but the tales we hear from officers returning from the various fronts and wishing to go to America confirm our suspicions that not many of them reach a "front," and my belief that Russia, as a factor of the war against Germany, has ceased to exist! From now on her military force and activity will become less and less. How can one help believing that this collapse, so helpful to Germany, is largely inspired and aided by that despicable country!

Just now we hear much of the "Kadets," a political party, and it will interest you to know where the name comes from. The initials of "Konstitutional Democrat" are

---

[22] This fortress was built soon after the founding of the city of St. Petersburg by Peter the Great in 1703. It not only served as a citadel for the city, but also as a prison. In the nineteenth century it housed many political prisoners, especially members of Russia's early revolutionary groups.

"K.D.", plural, "K.D.'s"; from those the word "Kadets" is simple. (In Russian "C" is pronounced as our "S", therefore "K" for "Constitutional." "D" is pronounced "day"). This party, which seems to include those most interested in what looks to us like a sane government, is in the lead, both in the Ministry and with the people. They are, just now, backed by the Cossacks, which materially strengthens their hands.

The trouble with all these political affairs in Russia is that, while today all seems serene and the Ship of State on a course for a safe harbor, tomorrow the entire situation may be reversed! I have never heard of such a kaleidoscopic control, and again my belief in German influence is strengthened, for every marked change is for the worse, as I see it; we are not permitted to congratulate ourselves for long at a time!

The "white nights" become more white; at midnight one can read ordinary newspaper print in the streets. Now we know why the heavy double curtains are at the windows and why one pair is so dark in color.

We have learned that an American Commission, headed by Mr. Elihu Root,[23] and composed of some of our noted men, will soon be in Petrograd. As a matter of fact we knew it a long time ago but were not supposed to mention it. Probably you knew all about it before we did. We are hoping great hope for if German and misguided Russian efforts are *properly* fought *now* it will mean much to the Allies. If only the enormity of the efforts required and the necessities to carry them out can be realized in the Capitals of the Allies, all may not yet be lost in Russia, but that looks like an impossibility, for those of us actually here can hardly realize today that what we *know* happened yesterday really took place. How much more difficult for those thousands of miles away and who have never seen Russia, to realize the conditions!

I promised to give you an outline of the Temporary Government here, but that will not be easy, since both personnel and policy change rapidly. On March 16th the new Government was formed, the Ministry being quite like the one under the Czar, though of course with different Ministers to replace those arrested by the revolutionists. Since then the Ministers have changed rather rapidly and it is useless to name all that have been in office; some of them are now in prison! Apparently it is unfortunate that the original Ministry could not have lasted longer, for I am assured that it contained "the best men in Russia." The principles of the Provisional Government, as published, and issued to the people, met with general approval and were adopted with the apparent intention of establishing a real government for and by the people. There were, of course, paragraphs intended to insure the safety of those who had made the success of the revolution possible, and there were small "jokers" indicating that the horny handed son of toil, whether or not he possessed ability, intended to help run

---

[23] Elihu Root (1845–1937) was the former US secretary of war and state who led a special commission, often referred to as the Root Commission, that was charged with investigating the economic and political situation in Russia in order to make recommendations to President Woodrow Wilson on ways that the United States could assist Russia. The United States supported the priority of the Allies on the Western Front.

the show. The personal safety of former political prisoners was also assured by the document which made no mention of any variety of offenses that might have made them prisoners.

Probably there was some distrust by the representatives of the soldiers and workmen, toward the Ministers, who were educated, and therefore in that class we hear so much of now in a despised manner as the "Bourjewie," by which they mean "Bourgeois." The Ministers, some of whom are still in office, were comparatively young and vigorous men who could have done very well, no doubt, in spite of inevitable mistakes if they had been permitted by the "Soldiers' and Workmen's Deputies" to really govern. It seems that the Ministers have never had any actual power and what they had is decreasing, the large body of men with the long name (above) permitting nothing of which they do not approve.

It is all very well to talk of a government by and for the people, but what exists here now is not that at all. It is a rule by a very few men who have *usurped* the power, and, from all I can learn, is very much more "autocratic" than the Czar's government ever became, also mostly inspired by hatred, more deadly and lacking many of the comforts obtainable under the old regime! Almost any reasonable advocate of a democratic form of government would become converted to Monarchy if forced to believe that Democracy means what we see here.

Among the original Ministers who are still in office, some with different portfolios, are: Prince Lvov[24] (President of the Council of Ministers), Nekrasov,[25] Kerensky,[26] Terestchenko.[27]

---

[24] Prince Georgy Lvov (1861–1925) was the head of the Provisional Government for several months after the abdication of Nicholas II.

[25] Nikolai V. Nekrasov (1879–1940) was minister of transport and minister of finance in the Provisional Government in 1917. In the decades after the revolution, he was arrested repeatedly and was finally executed in 1940, charged with participation in a Menshevik conspiracy.

[26] Alexander Kerensky (1881–1970) was head of the Provisional Government from February to October 1917. He was born in Simbirsk and his father had been the schoolmaster where Lenin and his brother attended school. Kerensky was unable to stabilize the political situation in the months that followed the collapse of the monarchy, and was toppled himself by the October Revolution. Fleeing Russia, he eventually settled in Paris, where he resided until World War II, when he moved to New York.

[27] Mikhail Tereshchenko (1886–1956) was briefly foreign minister for the Provisional Government in 1917. After being imprisoned in the Peter and Paul Fortress, he escaped and fled Russia. His family's name is associated with the famous Tereshchenko Diamond, which they brought to Russia from India. It is the largest blue diamond in the world (42.92 carats) and second largest diamond in the world, behind the Hope Diamond.

Guchkov and Miliukov,[28] probably best known and best liked, were also members but have been replaced. There are grounds for the belief that they could not put up with the insane interference of the "Soldiers' and Workmen's Deputies."

One great handicap, in addition to that interference, seems to result from the personal and party aspirations of some of the Ministers. The number of political parties is too large to consider enumerating it here, and probably will not permit any real concerted governmental action. When the desires of a Minister are thwarted he resigns; it would require either a very strong patriot or one with overwhelming personal ambitions to remain in the Ministry at the present time.

The *real* power is vested in a secret committee elected by the "Soldiers' and Workmen's Deputies" (I am beginning to dislike that term). That group with the long name is made up of nearly three thousand members presumably representing the classes named *in Russia*, but really representing those in and about Petrograd. A very large class, the Peasants, are only represented as some soldiers are peasants. The "S. & W. D." form a body too large to govern intelligently—too many personal interests are involved; it is too ignorant, selfish and brutal to really govern a country.

The various Army and Navy Commanders appointed by the Provisional Government, including the Commanders-in-Chief, have changed nearly as often as the Ministers; continuity of military policy in the war became impossible; military operations slacked up accordingly, and are still "slacking." I cannot find that, at any time since the revolution, there has been an authoritative expression *by the Government* as to the war against Germany. There have been nearly as many policies in this respect as there are political parties. The result seems inevitable.

I can learn of no real reason for the brutal excesses that took place during, immediately after and in the name of the Revolution. These were shown in their worst form and greatest extent at Kronstadt, but were general over the country; I suspect they resulted partly from hatred, individual and class, as well as from a condition that can be expressed as "drunk with power," or "intoxicated with freedom." Possibly the excesses show "the real nature of the beast."

It is evident that some officers, in times past, took advantage of the great power they had over their men; possibly this brought on a class hatred against the officers; evidence in this respect is conflicting, excellent observers stating that the feeling between the officers and men was all that could be desired, and other excellent observers stating that the officers were cruel and brutal; doubtless they were at times, but it is certain that many of the officers brutally tortured and murdered did not deserve their fate because they, individually, had mistreated their men.

---

[28] Pavel Milyukov (1859–1943) was a historian by training who served in the Third and Fourth Dumas, hoping to find a legal path to create a democratic government in Russia. By 1917, however, he had lost faith in Nicholas II and his ministers and supported the creation of the Provisional Government. He opposed the Bolshevik takeover in October and eventually left Russia, spending the remainder of his life in France.

"Election" of officers began after the success of the revolution was assured and it resulted in some ludicrous exhibitions; we see some of them daily. Committees in companies, regiments, armies, ships, divisions, fleets were formed to administer and direct them. The effect upon routine and efficiency need not be described.

Time presses and I must end this letter. Please pass it along as arranged. All of our love to you, our dear boy.

Affectionately,
Mother.

Kirochnaya, 8,
Petrograd,
June 12, 1917.

My dear Sister:

This is my first letter to you of the "family series" I promised to write from here. I shall assume that you receive all of them until I hear to the contrary. There is not much really new to write about, though I am seeing new things and hearing new details daily. The food difficulty is ever with us and Walter is now agitating the question of getting a supply of provisions from the United States before it is too late. It will only be a question of time when there will be practically no food and he wishes to anticipate such. There seems to be some difficulty in getting others to see that there will be a serious shortage, which is difficult to understand. We have begun to use the provisions we brought with us and Oh! how glad we are that we have them.

There is an effort (and it requires effort) to keep up some entertaining, there being but little else that can be done for recreation, and I am exceedingly glad that it is being done for it is the best way to meet the people; it is necessary to meet many if one is really to learn.

The usual number of wild rumors that is to be expected when a country is as upset as this one, are in circulation, but I find that there is generally some ground for a rumor. "Wild" things really happen and I do not wish to discourage anyone who relates them. There is a great deal going on in this unique effort to rebuild a nation and one cannot learn about them by staying at home and seeing no one.

It is necessary to meet and to talk to people from all over Russia as well as those in Petrograd, and for that reason Walter does not discourage the Russian officers from coming to see him with their requests to be sent to the United States, though he is not able to grant such requests. He keeps them in conversation, and asks them to come again to see him when they come to Petrograd. He finds many of them most congenial and while one cannot help feeling sympathy for them in their really serious condition, it is difficult to understand why they do not organize to rebuild their shattered military forces. There would be difficulties which would involve labor and danger, but to me it would be so much better to make the effort than to die as so many have died, by murder and suicide.

Dear little Miss Guerardhy, the interpreter, is quite winning our hearts and we find her family, consisting of father, mother and brother, very attractive also. They are all very brave under circumstances that would quite warrant despair; heretofore they have lived in luxury, all their lives, and they have *not* been drones who, possibly, deserve punishment for their sins, as most likely some Russians who occupied high places in the past have deserved and are getting.

Strikes and economic failures continue and grow all over Russia, while the conditions in the Army and Navy become steadily worse.

I have given a dinner party! "That is not an unusual thing for you to do," I hear you say. But it *is,* when you consider that I have been in Russia about a month and my four servants speak and understand not a word of any language but their own. The necessity for so many servants in a comparatively small apartment results from the requirements of the many bread lines, or rather "lines" for whatever one gets for the household. There must be at least one servant in these "queues" at all times in order to get the few items that are sold in the shops and we find we get more if we have two representatives making purchases for us! Many well-dressed ladies, officers of high rank and servants make up these lines. Here again the resignation is noticeable.

There are lines for bread, meat, fish, milk, butter, eggs, kerosene, candles, etc., and it is a sad sight to see the shop closed—sold out—and that part of the line which had not reached the door melt away with looks sadly dejected to join another line at a distant shop. There are cards for all such commodities and the purchasers can only buy what the card calls for, though having a card does not insure ability to make a purchase!

We were made happy by the receipt of a small mail this week but it is distressing to read in our daily papers and in the magazines what is being published in the United States about Russia! There is a strict censorship which I must not violate in writing to you, but I may say that you need not believe any glowing accounts you read to the effect that Russia is maintaining a continued activity in the war, nor of the arrival in Petrograd of any Russian Napoleons. Probably the censorship is partly responsible for the erroneous accounts we read; possibly nothing else would pass the censor.

Speaking of Napoleons—Ministers come and go rapidly but no one has yet deserved such a title and I am beginning to fear there is not, among these millions of Russians, one who can "save Russia." That expression is used often by our Russian friends:—"How can we save Russia!" "Why don't the Allies save Russia!" "Why doesn't the United States do something to save Russia!" "Why do you send troops to France; why don't you send them to save Russia?" These and many similar difficult questions are asked and are hard to answer, more particularly when all the Allied Military and Naval Attaches are working hard over the same problems. Walter has been trying since the second week of his duty here to get an agreement for a few reliable Allied troops to be sent here and save the day, to endeavor to restore the morale. The size of the force needed will increase with every delay, and the necessity seems so urgent.

The Root Commission is due here tomorrow and its presence means a busy time for our Embassy. Many of us are also hoping it means a clear conception in Washington, hence in other Capitals of our Allies, of the real situation here, its dangers, necessities and cure. I mean the dangers to the Allies.

I have met several times a charming little Russian woman, Madame Vacquier, whose husband is an officer at the front and who herself spent two years at the front as a Red Cross nurse. She has seen Russian armies victorious, and in flight; she has many interesting and instructive photographs and narratives concerning her experiences, and it is from such persons that a stranger can get a clear conception of Russian character. Aside from her fund of interest about the war, she is delightful company and I am sure we shall be good friends.

We are still "apartment hunting" for the rightful occupants of this apartment say positively they will return. They have not asked my advice, so they will not receive it, but I *am* in a position to advise *you* not to visit Russia at this time, nor for some time to come.

I am so sorry I missed seeing Russia when it was comfortable and safe to travel. It is, of course, a wonderful and rich country, with many places of natural and artificial beauty and interest, but it is a real labor to travel now. Thousands of soldiers roam over the country and crowd the few trains. Even in Petrograd it is scarcely possible to use the street cars, for they are crowded to three times their normal capacity. Soldiers (who do not pay fare) fill the cars and cling to all available places outside. Why more of them are not hurt I cannot understand, for I have even seen them standing on the ends of the axles, holding on with their hands in the windows. They do not seem to be going to any particular place; they ride for a while in one direction, see a car going at right angles and rush to cling on that one. Many have never before been in Petrograd; they wish to see it.

I never imagined I would see so many idle men! Thousands of men in uniform doing nothing but sit on benches in the few parks and eat sunflower seeds! When the pocketful of seeds disappears (the bench is then surrounded by the shells) he decides he will take a street car ride; if the car passes a railroad station he decides he will go someplace by train (any place will do); he has no ticket and there is no room for him, but he goes; the train stops at a station he has never seen before; he decides he will visit that village! More and more I become impressed with the childish minds of these soldiers. On the other hand, when I hear of the horrible things the peasants and the soldiers do to the owners of estates as well as to the estates themselves I wonder how such children can think of all the horrible details; then I remember how unintentionally cruel a dear little girl can be to a kitten and it all seems more simple.

Of some of the details I hear I cannot write you; possibly I can tell you some day. The tongues of cattle are cut out to spite the owners; animals are skinned alive for the same purpose; beautiful paintings are cut and slashed because the peasant can see no use for them; other works of art destroyed for the same reason. Yet, with all this and worse going on in Russia, I feel a peculiar sensation of safety, and have no fear—though I am not a brave person at all. To be sure there still remains a certain amount of respect for foreigners which is evident, but the most of us are in that despised "Bourjewie" class and the respect will not last.

A Russian mob is easily swayed. The Germans, who undoubtedly know Russia better than do the Allies, will not continue to permit the Allies to be safe in Russia any longer than it pleases them to do so. And, by the way, the strict ban on the German language which was in effect when we arrived is now a dead issue; of course there has been no decree issued permitting its use, but we hear it on the streets and nothing happens. There is a story told, and believed by many, that a gentleman in Petrograd was fined a few months ago for speaking in German to his dog!

It is late by the clock, but still daylight; it is quite light all night now but we manage to have air *and* darkness in which to sleep. We send our best greetings, regards and love.

Affectionately yours,

Chapter III
THE ROOT COMMISSION

Kirochnaya, 8,
Petrograd,
June 19th.

My dear—:

    I am beginning to fear that my weekly letters will begin to have a sameness, in spite of all that is happening in this wonderful country! However, I will continue them until my conscience prevents, then I will increase the length of time between them.

    The Commission headed by Mr. Root arrived on the day set, June 13th, and took up its quarters in the Winter Palace. Living there, the members will not become impressed with any hardships I am certain and glad. I have begun to have Thursday afternoons at home, and am so happy, for our Russian friends come to drink tea with me. Walter has been very busy, with others of the Embassy Staff and members of the Root Commission who are learning all they can of Russia, each in his own department. I spend more and more time at the Lazaret and even bring sewing home with me. There is so much that can be done and there are so few of us to do it.

    The weather has improved greatly and is as beautiful as one could wish. We enjoy the relief from the shivering sensations the need for fuel economy forced us to endure. I am told it grows very hot in Petrograd in summer and that most of our friends will go to cooler Finland, but I doubt whether Walter will be able to get away for more than a few days at a time. We received a large mail since I last wrote, with fine letters from all of the family. I think I never before appreciated mail from home as I do here! I am again a temporary widow for Walter has gone to Sevastopol with Admiral Glennon[1] to visit the Black Sea Fleet. In the meantime there are many social happenings, many of them connected with the presence here of the Commission, and there are many new sights to see.

    One of the most wonderful things to me in Russia is the church singing—I cannot hear enough of it. There are many churches in Petrograd and one, very near our apartment, I pass frequently. If the choir is singing I always stop to listen. I have only heard male voices, but am told there are, at Christmas time, more wonderful mixed choirs. The Russian music of all kinds appeals to me strongly and I grow more sorry

---

[1] Admiral James H. Glennon (1857–1940) was an American naval officer who served on the Root Commission.

each day that so much of the beauty and charm of this country is being destroyed—it is a very sad thought.

Political affairs have been very quiet and I hear better news from the various fronts. I wonder the presence of the American Mission is not a restraining influence that will quiet matters temporarily! The anarchists are beginning to show themselves and to make their presence felt. The number of street corner groups and orators has recently been on the increase. We hear that a large force of Cossacks is near the city, ready to prevent disorder. Why do you suppose the mob fears the Cossacks so, while all of my friends, of whatever nationality, are so glad to know they are about? Must be a good reason for so general a feeling on the part of both groups!

Our usual conversation embraces much of *food*, revolution, counter-revolution, Provisional Government, Soldiers' and Workmen's Deputies, anarchists, and the high cost of living, until it grows somewhat monotonous.

I am a little uneasy about those who went to Sevastopol, for we hear rumors that the Kronstadt Headquarters, containing always the worst elements, has sent delegates to Sevastopol, hoping, in the absence of the loyal men stationed there with the Committee, of which I wrote some time ago, to stir up strife. That Committee from the Black Sea Fleet is now touring the country, in an effort to keep Russia in the war and to inspire their comrades to keep up the fight against Germany. It would be too bad indeed if, because of their absence on this patriotic mission, their own comrades, heretofore the most dependable in all Russia, should become contaminated by the emissaries from Kronstadt! Doesn't it all look like the evil hand of Germany!

Sunday, June 24th.

I was prevented from writing more on the nineteenth and have been very busy since. Walter surprised me by returning home yesterday from Sevastopol. He left again tonight for Archangel. I saw but little of him but he confirmed the rumors, the bad news, from Sevastopol. The night before his party arrived the soldiers, sailors and workmen there decided to "dismiss" Vice-Admiral Kolchak,[2] the Commander-in-Chief of the Black Sea Fleet. They "dismissed" him and he gave up his command at three o'clock in the morning. One never knows what is best in such cases, but many believe it would have been better for Russia if Admiral Kolchak had gathered a few of his loyal supporters and defied those who dismissed him—if he had declined to be "dismissed." Probably there would have been bloodshed—possibly not! Now there will *certainly* be a repetition of the horrors that have taken place elsewhere when the lawless took control. While Walter was in Sevastopol he saw "committees" of sailors

---

[2] Alexander Kolchak (1874–1920) was an admiral in the Imperial Russian Navy who, after the revolution, became the acknowledged leader of the anti-Bolshevik White forces in the Russian Civil War and established an anti-Bolshevik rival government in Siberia. As the White movement fell apart, however, he was captured and executed by the Bolsheviks in 1920.

visiting officers' quarters on shore and demanding (and receiving) their side arms. Some officers broke their swords before surrendering them; one committed suicide rather than submit to the disgrace.

The American Admiral and his party were met when they arrived at Sevastopol by three Russian Naval Officers, a *sailor*, and a *workman* who is described as having been dirty, unshaven and horrid looking. It did not require many minutes for the party of Americans to learn how the land lay! The sailor and workman had been detailed by the "Soldiers' and Workmen's Deputies" of Sevastopol as a part of the reception committee, and these two accompanied the American officers everywhere, eating luncheon and dinner with them at the Naval Officers' Club, and otherwise making nuisances of themselves. What a state of affairs!

The American officers visited some of the ships, probably as a matter of form, and were glad after luncheon to go in an automobile to Balaclava, driving through the famous "Valley of Death" and refreshing their history of the Crimean War. They were much impressed by a panorama painting of the Battle of Sevastopol, which is appropriately displayed in a large circular house in the park and is very beautiful. At dinner that night the party was joined by another workman, who reported that, as a result of two short speeches made by the American Admiral, the Sevastopol Soldiers' and Workmen's Deputies had voted to rescind all their obnoxious orders of the day before *except* the dismissal of Admiral Kolchak. I wonder what they voted the day after the Americans left!

It has grown exceedingly hot and I now understand why we are advised to leave Petrograd during summer. I probably will not be able to leave, in spite of the heat!

Mrs. Pankhurst[3] is here from England to see if she can help Russia through the Russian women. I have met her at tea and at a Russian Women's Club, and find her to be a very interesting woman, not at all the type many have pictured her—she is sweet and womanly as well as being most intelligent. She gives us the sad news that our Ally, France, is growing very weak, and it seems that only the arrival of American forces in large numbers can save her. Our faith in our country permits us to believe that France will be saved!

There have been receptions to the members of the Root Commission who remain in Petrograd and I am glad to attend them to meet more people and to learn what occurs! My head is so full now, and I wish so hard that all of you at home could see things as they *are* here, that I am in a *whirl*. A peculiar arrangement was forced upon me when I engaged ice. I had to pay for a month in advance, and they promise to deliver *if they can*! This form of government is certainly for *some* of the people—the

---

[3] Emmeline Pankhurst (1858–1928) was a British feminist and suffragette who helped women get the right to vote in Great Britain. Though criticized for her militant tactics, which included vandalism and hunger strikes, she has been recognized as a critical figure in the women's suffrage movement.

iceman for example. The Embassy received some flour—our share is twenty-three pounds and I was glad to get it.

Tonight had my first view of the Northern Lights and I will never forget the beautiful sight! There are many beautiful things in Russia—what a shame they must be accompanied by so much disorder and suffering!

Now must stop and get some sleep. Appropriate greetings to all!

Faithfully yours,

Kirochnaya, 8,
Petrograd,
July 1, 1917.

My dear—:

Another busy week has passed, both for Russia and for me. Walter has been to Archangel and is back in Petrograd. He tells me the conditions of travel on those railroads are like what he found on the roads leading south. The Admiral and his party traveled in the private car of the Minister of War and Navy, so they escaped the crowding of the remainder of the trains, and were as comfortable as possible, but the rest of the train! And all trains they saw! *Packed* with humanity; soldiers riding on the roofs, steps and platforms of all the cars! He quite convinces me that I must not travel at this time, for it would be quite inconvenient to get out of a compartment by way of the window, there being no other practicable exit, and when I tried to reenter find that my place was more than occupied by soldiers!

I have again visited the Bazaar, called by some the "Jews' Market" and by others the "Thieves' Market." There are many bargains to be had there but I cannot run the risk of having a friend say, "Where did you get my rug?" Robberies have increased in number, but this is not to be wondered at. There is no police force and the thieves know nothing will happen to them unless they are unfortunate enough to be caught in the act by a group of temporarily right-minded, when they would be torn to pieces; this is a *remote* possibility! Many jewels, pieces of valuable plate, rugs, pieces of handsome furniture, works of art, in fact everything to furnish a house and clothe one's self is to be found in the Bazaar, all having come from some handsome apartments or palaces, but I cannot bring myself to buy and thus profit by the misfortunes of others. Many of the articles have been pawned, of course, by those who have now no income and must sell their belongings in order to buy food.

I have met frequently the woman "Colonel" of the much advertised "Woman's Battalion." She is full of zeal, and hopes sincerely that by this movement of woman soldiers to the front the men will be made ashamed of their conduct in running away. I have watched the women recruits drilling at their barracks and marching in the streets; I have also observed the loafing men soldiers (though they do not seem to be real men, nor are they soldiers for any other reason than that they wear a uniform!)

looking on and passing rude jests. I am convinced the "Woman's Battalion" will not accomplish the excellent purpose for which it was patriotically started, but the faces of the drilling and marching women furnish a study; their determination and purpose is evident from their serious and exalted expressions; I have yet to see a smile on one face. I so dislike to feel as I do—that they will accomplish nothing.

There are now daily reports of clashes between different political groups, sometimes accompanied by the use of force, and always the more disorderly element wins; a certain terrorism, inspired by what they have done and will do is their strongest weapon and ally. If the presence of the Root Commission had a restraining effect it is decreasing. Members of the Commission are in different parts of Russia, learning what they can of the real conditions, but there are many conditions which can only be learned by "keeping house," and those they will not learn. I am learning them, but have a certain feeling that my knowledge will only be of use in Russia; also, the knowledge is only of use here when accompanied by considerable philosophy!

Now I have myself heard the cry "The Cossacks are coming" and have seen its effect on the mob. I was in a crowded street where many groups were being harangued by orators, when some practical joker started the cry. There actually were no Cossacks coming, but the danger of being trampled by that fearful mob in its rush to get clear of the imagined Cossacks was almost as great as if they had actually appeared and were riding us down. The looks of abject fear and terror that I saw on the faces will remain in my memory for a long time.

Walter found that military conditions in the north were better than those with which we are now quite familiar hereabouts simply because fewer officers have been murdered. However, there is no discipline, therefore no military or naval force worth considering. The food problem is also grave; they had difficulty in supplying meals in their private car. They have now been to the Black Sea and to the White Sea—I am wondering what color they will visit next—it will be RED, wherever it is!

We have been offered the beautiful apartment of Mr. and Mrs. McA. Smith,[4] a charming American couple who expect to leave here about the time we must give up this apartment. We will be fortunate indeed if we can get theirs for it is attractively located on the Neva, next door to the French Embassy, and is furnished in exquisite taste and beauty. It is large, too, and will give us exactly what we want most. My days at home here are growing as my acquaintances increase in number and I will be glad to occupy a larger home.

We have seen another interesting phase of Russian character; heard a pitiful wailing and observed three women who might have been the mother, wife and daughter of a departing soldier and who were showing every sign of intense grief, except that they were absolutely dry-eyed—not a tear to be seen! A Russian friend was with

---

[4] Crosley is referring to L. McAllister Smith, a prominent businessman with the Guaranty Trust Company of New York, and his wife. After the Smiths left Russia, the Crosleys occupied their apartment.

us and I commented upon the unusual sight. He said "That is nothing—these women weep very easily—doubtless they are glad he is going away and they will be laughing before he is out of sight!" They were.

Mr. Root and members of his Commission visited our Lazaret where all those who have worked so hard were assembled to meet them. The actual hospital activities of the Lazaret are on the wane! Wounded are not arriving in Petrograd now for very obvious reasons. The hospital was established for wounded Russian soldiers; we are beginning to ask how long we may properly maintain it under existing conditions. The sewing and the work connected with its upkeep must continue as long as we keep it open, but the spirit of mutiny is extending and even wounded soldiers are beginning to believe that they are "free" to do entirely as they wish, regardless of necessary hospital regulations. Some private hospitals have been obliged to close on that account. "Our" soldiers still remain "good" and we will keep it open as long as possible.

This Sunday morning being as perfect as weather ever gets and all seeming quiet in our neighborhood, we decided to go to the Kazan Cathedral,[5] on the Nevsky Prospect, where a special service in honor of Mr. Root and his associates was to be held. We started to walk to the Cathedral and were congratulating ourselves upon the beauty of the day and the total absence of disorder. While thus pleasantly engaged we came to a cordon of polite but firm soldiers; much above the average in appearance, cleanliness and manner, but who positively refused to yield to my smiling appeals for permission to pass; even the heretofore sesame of "Amerikansky Posolstvo" (from the American Embassy) failed in effect. We saw great crowds on the Field of Mars but were too far away to determine what was going on. One of the cordons who really seemed somewhat inclined to be nice, only he would not let us pass, advised us to follow one of the canals, take another street, and gain the Nevsky higher up. We started, but soon ran into another cordon through which we could not pass; a more roundabout way was selected and soon we were in sight of the Nevsky, though some distance from the Cathedral, and all seemed serene and normal.

But! Just around the corner we were about to turn came the "put-put-put-put-pp-pp-pp puuuuuuttttt" with which our ears had become somewhat familiar as the music of the machine gun. People in a stampede came tearing down the street where we were, their faces indicating great terror, and reminding me of what I had seen when "The Cossacks are coming" was shouted. The faces of two women, in particular, I shall not forget; one was carrying a small bottle of milk, something very precious now and hard to get, and her look seemed to be more one of terror lest the milk be spilled than for her own safety; the other was carrying a bundle and dragging a small child; her wildness seemed to be inspired by the necessity to save the child; the two

---

[5] Built between 1801 and 1811, Kazan Cathedral is a spectacular cathedral on Nevsky Prospect, the main street that runs through the heart of St. Petersburg.

expressions were alike, yet different, while both showed more fear than I have ever seen similarly expressed.

We slipped into a large open doorway, Walter placing me behind a soldier who was on guard there and at whom we smiled in a *very* friendly manner, where I was out of the more or less dangerous human current, then looked out to find all serene again, no "put-put-ting" at all, and the woman with her precious milk returning toward the Nevsky as though nothing had happened. The time could not have been more than two or three minutes between her departure from that street in great fear and her return to it quite calm. A Russian gentleman who had joined us in our efforts to pass cordons volunteered to go to the near corner of the Nevsky and see what all the excitement was about. He returned with the report that all seemed quiet and we again started for the Cathedral, but, on the Nevsky again ran into a line of soldiers through which we could not pass and around which there seemed to be no means of reaching our destination. We walked back to our apartment, better for the exercise on this beautiful day, sorry to miss the special service, and quite convinced that Petrograd is "difficult"!

Tonight I became a temporary widow again; Walter leaves to visit the naval forces around the Baltic. If anyone had told me I could, without dying of fright, remain for nights alone in a large apartment on the *ground floor*, with only Russian servants upon whom to depend, with the greatest disorders going on, I should have considered that person not well informed as to my bravery! It is a fact I have done just these things, am still alive, and have not even been badly frightened; I cannot understand myself at all! I have more reason to be uneasy right now than I have ever had in my life but I am going to bed and sleep. Good Night!

Affectionately yours,

Kirochnaya, 8,
Petrograd,
July 7, 1917.

My dear—

Somehow I am too busy to do those things I wish most to do! I hope my meaning is clear to you, it is not quite clear to me! The necessities grow monotonous, for it is really a struggle to live here. Yet, there is so much of interest that I would not leave if I could. Possibly a man would say the foregoing proves I am a woman!

Walter has been to Revel, Riga Gulf, Helsingfors, and other points in the Baltic, and has returned. He reports a very interesting trip, but a sad one inasmuch as he is now fully convinced that the Russian Navy, as a fighting machine, no longer exists! He heard many of the sad details of cruelty and murder of which I have briefly written you and now he *knows* that Russia is out of this war, only to be brought back by efforts too great for the Allies to realize as necessary or attempt to make.

There is an undercurrent here, plainly evident, but not possible for a stranger to trace, and impossible to describe, indicating that we may expect an upheaval before very long. I know of meetings, drilling, propaganda and accumulation of arms that can only mean one thing. When that thing will happen, no one not in the "meetings" can tell. Matters do not remain at a standstill; they grow worse each day, but it is only after a few days have passed that comparisons can be made. The price of everything that is for sale (not a large variety!) has soared almost beyond belief, but one has only to attempt to make a purchase to believe.

While walking on the Nevsky with an interpreter, among the thousands of idly strolling soldiers, we heard a substantial looking woman say "I have lost two sons in this war and I want these idle soldiers to go to the front instead of staying in Petrograd and eating all the bread!" The numerous street crowds being addressed by men and women, as well as the indoor anarchistic meetings, have greatly increased in numbers. Now I can begin to understand what they are talking about, and I hear one orator arguing for a continuance of Russia in the war, and another affirming loudly that war is not necessary and must cease. The fact is that Russians will now continue to kill each other, but will *cease killing Germans*! How childish are the Russians and how fiendishly clever are the Germans!

We could overcome their cleverness if we were to make sufficient effort but effort costs time and money and force; it first of all requires understanding at the sources of power and money, and we despair! Why am I not blessed with millions in money! They could be used here now to a better advantage than at any other place in this upset world of ours! There are many Americans here who are doing all they can, but there are too few, and they are too poorly equipped to stem the tide that is not only bringing Russia to her ruin, to the detriment of the world, but will cost the United States and our *Allies thousands of lives and millions in wealth.*

I saw a wonderful sky over the Neva last week. It was streaked with a vivid pink, with a grayish haze lower down, seeming to envelop the steeples, roofs and dome on the opposite side of the Neva. (The political atmosphere is surcharged with evidences of terrors to come and even the elements seem to try and portray them. I am not superstitious but with the permanent threat now existing, I am likely to assign unlikely meanings to those things which are quite natural.) At the same time I saw the moon rise, and I wondered if the moon had grown since I saw it full the last time! It was so large and brilliant! It looked like burnished silver—not the same moon at all with which I am familiar!

Everybody was kind to me while my husband was away and I was taken by the Ambassador and others to the few entertainments that were given. Many friends came to see me and had me to dine. I also had several here for luncheon, tea and dinner. It is not a healthy atmosphere in which to be alone and I am fortunate to have so many friends. We have been invited to visit with a delightful Russian couple, a

Naval Commander and his wife, on Oesel Island.[6] It would be a charming "holiday" but I do not see how we can accept. Walter believes it will only be a question of time, probably before winter begins, when the Germans will decide they want that island and others around Riga Gulf. I do not wish to be there when they capture it, for I have heard too much of the acts that are committed by defeated Russian soldiers and sailors!

The Ambassador gave a reception on July Fourth which was attended by all Americans as well as many of other nationalities. It would have amused, (and probably also have disgusted) you to see the maneuvers of *certain* people to attract attention to themselves! It takes all kinds of people to make a world, but those who believe they can only advance by pushing others behind can well be dispensed with. And that principle, by the way, is the one influencing the Russians now seeking power. We heard of much "pushing behind" (which includes everything, even murder) but we fail to observe an advance in any particular.

Mrs. Smith, whose apartment we expect to occupy, arranged a meeting at the hotel Astoria, where Mrs. Pankhurst could address those interested and where all could express their views, with the object in view of starting some Allied Propaganda to overcome that being spread by the Germans. Mrs. Pankhurst is a most interesting and attractive speaker, who fully understands her subject. The object of the meeting is a most worthy one, but one that Governments, not individuals, should take up, the reason being that the task is too great for individuals.

We continue our sewing at the Lazaret which reminds me—yesterday an incident occurred which cheered us considerably. One wounded soldier who had been cared for there and who had been discharged as cured, some days ago, returned yesterday and told the others who are still being treated that they were free, did not have to obey hospital regulations, and advised them to mutiny. The wounded soldiers, without other inspirations than their own feelings, ordered him to leave the hospital immediately. If only such feelings could be generally invoked! We are so few!

The Root Commission begins to talk of leaving, and we are sorry, for their presence inspires hope. Numerous Allied conferences are taking place and everyone is working hard for the good of Russia, but even our wonderful railroad men who are now here feel that they will be prevented from carrying out reform *by Russians*. What a country for intrigue!

We are hearing more and more of Mr. Kerensky, and less of other members of the Ministry. As might be expected, many damaging tales are circulated concerning this man who is becoming prominent. In the absence (apparently) of anyone else to lead, I am hoping Kerensky will be able to do it, but some of his speeches seem

---

[6] Oesel Island was an important defensive port that kept the Gulf of Riga closed to the Germans through most of 1917.

hysterical, and some of his orders, particularly as they relate to the Army, show him to be anything but practical. I hope he is not as false as some stories of him indicate!

There are some parts of the Navy remaining "good." Recently some ("good") submarines lined up some ("bad") battleships at Helsingfors and the crews of the submarines informed the crews of the battleships they would sink said battleships if the crews thereof did not behave themselves and cease threatening the Commander-in-Chief. This is a perfectly true story and indicates the condition of the Russian Navy in the Baltic. (I omit similar stories that I do not believe to be true.) The crews of some destroyers decided at a meeting that they were not satisfied with the way matters were going in Petrograd. They "voted" to go and bombard Petrograd, thereby administering what they believed to be a much needed rebuke. They required their officers to assemble with them and ordered them to conduct their vessels to Petrograd for bombarding purposes. The officers declined. The men said, "Very well, we will get other officers to take us and we will kill you." This shows the disposition of "free Russian sailors." And so it goes—no one knows how far it will go. We have been wondering where all the money came from, for it is in evidence among the soldiers and sailors. Now we believe we know, for I am creditably informed that Russian money was once made in Germany. This method of making war was used by Napoleon, and I suspect the German General Staff is not less cunning than he was!

The food and fuel situation continues to grow worse, though this is said to be the best month for both. However, it not being a good season for transportation, we can't get the food and fuel. We have received some few small packages of food from the States, and Oh! how welcome they are!

With love and affection to all.

Faithfully yours,

Chapter IV
A REVOLUTION!

Kirochnaya, Vosyem
Petrograd,
July 18, 1917

My dear Aunt Nell:

This time there is so much to tell you I hardly know where to begin. The Root Commission left (Monday, July 9th). As one of the most interesting things that has happened to me, Mr. and Mrs. McA. Smith called one afternoon and brought me *ten eggs*! That is *real* friendship, but it is also a gift that is beyond my power to return in kind or value. Ten eggs were worth more to me at that particular time than ten dollars! We all went to the station to say "Good-bye" to the Commission when it left and took advantage of the opportunity to look in the train of the former Czar, which had been turned over for the use of the Commission. It is a truly luxurious train and I wish I could travel in it. Some of the rooms are very large and beautifully furnished; some of the staterooms are double. I was interested in the table upon which the abdication was signed, and particularly in the tastefully decorated rooms formerly occupied by the children of the Czar.

We began to hear unpleasant rumors of an uprising immediately after the departure of Mr. Root, and we actually saw the anarchists drilling. It was done openly and anyone wishing to see it could do so. One does not stop routine when rumors of trouble begin. There would be no routine if we did that! We had an opportunity to hear what had been called the Imperial Orchestra and I am very glad we went; I am more than ever in love with Russian music. It was really wonderful! I even gave another dinner party!

Four of the Embassy Secretaries and Attaches took a beautiful palace "over on the Islands" (across the Neva), the Russian owner of which was very anxious to have it occupied by Americans in order that it might be protected from the mobs. Just before they took possession one of them learned it was about to be seized by the anarchistic soldiers; he hastily secured an American flag, jumped into an automobile and managed to reach the palace just in time to hoist the flag before the soldiers arrived. They grumbled some, but went away; the respect for foreigners not yet having entirely disappeared. We dined there recently and it almost makes me ill to think of those unclean soldiers occupying such a beautiful home; they actually are occupying similar ones.

We have received our first mail in more than a month. That is a very unpleasant feature of our stay here. We have spent a day at Sestroretsk, a charming seaside resort near Finland, where one of my Russian friends, Madame Vacquier, has a cottage. It was a relief to get out of the heat *and tension* of the city. They use the beach wagon-bath-houses there, drawn in and out of the water by a horse which seemed to enjoy his part of the fun very much. I had not before the convenience of getting into a bath house fully dressed, on dry land and being taken to sea while getting into a bathing suit, with the reverse operation when tired of swimming. Sestroretsk is in and surrounded by a vast pine grove and the pine laden air, straight from the sea acts like a stimulant. We had luncheon and dinner with my friend, coming into Petrograd late at night, sorry we could not stay there and willing not to see a soldier for a month.

There are a few bridge parties these days and we play as often as convenient. Our friends are beginning to dread going out at night and no one seems to have time to play cards by day; it is about the only recreation possible now, and with the never absent tense atmosphere in which we live, recreation is probably as great a necessity as it is for those actually at the front.

Monday night, the sixteenth, Walter was working in his office and I was in the drawing room translating a receipt from English into Russian, in order that my very good cook could give us some real American biscuits if we get flour. The doorbell rang and I heard a man in my husband's office, talking earnestly. As there are many visitors of that sort I thought nothing of it, but soon he came in and said quietly, "Please put your most valuable small things in a bag and be ready to leave for the Embassy in five minutes!" I said, (of course!) "Why?"—when he told me to look out of the window. There they were!!! *Hundreds* of the worst looking armed men I ever expect to see, coming up our street! The rumors were being confirmed and trouble was upon us.[1]

You should have seen me hurry! I had heard the noise of tramping feet, but there are several barracks on our street and often soldiers in considerable numbers pass, either in ranks or just wandering along, so the noise did not interest me. The gentleman who called was a Russian aviator, an officer, who some weeks ago came to ask Walter to send him to the United States to join our forces. We had him for luncheon with us and he has been here several times to call.

Monday evening he arrived from Moscow in civilian clothes (as a disguise), and was met at the station by his orderly who told him what was going to happen that night. He immediately took an ezevoschick and hurried to our house, telling us there

---

[1] Crosley is describing what is usually called the "July Crisis," when soldiers, sailors, and industrial workers took to the streets of Petrograd in spontaneous demonstrations against the Provisional Government. Many of the demonstrators were armed and the situation was violent and dangerous.

would be a big fight and much of it would take place on our corner! We did not believe it until the head of the column appeared, when he remembered that in the big revolution this corner had been a very bloody spot, and he asked me to get ready to leave for the Embassy. The Russian officer insisted upon accompanying us there, saying he could talk to the anarchists in their own language, and, because of the way in which he was dressed, he could make them believe he was one of them, so we left, telling our servants to follow us; by the time we could get out of our front door the street in front of the house was *filled* with the dangerous looking creatures and we had to face them as we went out! UGH!!

At the Embassy not a word had been heard of the uprising but soon members of the Staff began to arrive with reports of the same nature from all parts of the city, as well as fighting in some parts, and very soon we could hear the firing from many directions. Scouts were constantly leaving the Embassy and returning to report conditions. Walter counted seven thousand in the column that passed our house and from the various reports turned in at the Embassy it was estimated that there were at least seventy thousand armed workmen and soldiers in charge of the city that night. In addition there were the ever present auto trucks full of men, rifles and machine guns, and they dashed merrily about, on their joy-riding terrorism bent.

I saw one automobile "commandeered" (which is a polite term here for "stolen"). It was quite near the Embassy, as we were on our way from our house. A group of armed men simply took the car and climbed in. It was a limousine, so they broke all the glass in order that their rifles might project in a more satisfying manner! I saw another in which the glass at the back had been smashed in order to permit the muzzle of a machine gun to show itself. Of course the gun pointed to the heavens, but it looked well there and could make a noise pointing upward as well as in any other direction! Besides, the bullets would come down some place, and were just as likely to kill women and children as though they had been from an aimed gun!

These were the anarchists, the Leninites, the ones who had been drilling "on the Islands," and Lenin is the one who came here through Germany, with a special permit from the German Government, and was permitted to enter Russia. Had Germany a hand in this? Well, after Walter had made several scouting trips from the Embassy he finally telephoned to the Embassy from our apartment, saying he would come for me and we would spend the rest of the night at home. About one o'clock in the morning I left the Embassy, escorted by six of the younger men of the Staff, who insisted that they would "see us safely home." We were about two blocks from the Embassy when we ran into *hundreds* of marching, singing anarchists! We went on, and the marchers passed our home as we went in the door, darkened our windows, made a dim light and had some refreshments, including some fudge I had made with chocolate and sugar from Vancouver. We were in bed by two o'clock, and slept well, with no disturbances.

The next day, Tuesday the seventeenth, there was really not much excitement (for Petrograd). While we were at breakfast a few thousand workmen, women and children marched past our windows singing—most Russians sing as they march—their red banners notifying those interested that they wanted bread. Machine gun and rifle shots could be heard nearly all day, and just as we were about to sit down for luncheon they began at our popular corner and it sounded as if they were firing in our windows, but they were not. The sight on the street was one long to be remembered, with men, women, children, horses, all going as fast as they could, away from the shooting, which did not last long, and after it finished the street was quickly filled again as though nothing had happened. We ate luncheon in our bedroom, that room being the one most protected from bullets!

During a lull in the fighting, that afternoon, Mr. and Mrs. McA. Smith came to see us; shortly after they arrived our corner again became a battlefield, with the most violent firing we had yet heard. Our friends stayed for dinner but took advantage of the next lull to get to their home, only about six minutes of brisk walking from our apartment. They telephoned their safe arrival and said they had passed through the "battlefield" and had counted sixteen dead horses in the street, with men, killed and wounded, in a nearby church. The horses were not all removed for several days, and the killed were the Cossacks who had driven the anarchists across the Neva. We learned that the firing was all done by the anarchists, the Cossacks having charged with knouts only.

During the day the rumors of trouble in Finland were confirmed and I believe, officially, Finland is no longer a part of Russia. If the Finns can establish law and order they are fortunate in their freedom from Russia, for it will be many a moon before there is peace, plenty, law and order in this country, rich though it is.

Today we got additional details of the fighting everywhere last night, and, as usual, an intelligent estimate of the number of killed cannot be given! The net result is that the anarchists have been driven out of this part of the city and are again at their headquarters across the Neva, defying the Provisional Government, which, in its representatives, is now difficult to locate. Lenin, on his arrival here, commandeered (still polite) and was permitted to do so, the beautiful and magnificently furnished palace of a former Court favorite, a ballet dancer, and that is where his headquarters are now. I have talked with a Russian officer who has been in it since being occupied by Lenin and his "staff." He tells the usual story of wanton destruction, filth and lack of appreciation of the art in the palace.

The end is not yet, for these anarchists know they captured Petrograd in a night, and, though the Provisional Government took it back, opening all the draws in the bridges across the Neva except one, to keep the Leninites away from the city, it is not so far across the Neva, after all, and they will "come back." They organized, drilled openly, scattered propaganda, accumulated arms and ammunition, and otherwise planned to capture Petrograd, which most Russians consider to be Russia, before this premature effort. *We* knew they were doing all this, so of course the Provisional Government knew it. Why did they not stop it? Is it because there is a traitor (or more than one) in *that* camp? This effort, which has temporarily failed, was made because many of the Cossacks who were hereabouts to preserve law and order, were sent to Finland to put down the uprising there. A very few remaining Cossacks were sufficient to drive back the many thousands of anarchists *this time*. Who will drive them back the next time?

This letter is too long, but—!
Always yours,
Affectionately,

Kirochnaya, 8,
Petrograd,
July 26, 1917.

My dear—

There is so much to tell you, so much I can't tell you, and so little time in which to tell you what I can! I wish I had a stenographer; my brain works so much faster than my fingers!

When we first arrived here we learned that a Constituent Assembly, elected by all Russia, would soon meet and prepare a constitution and form of government for the country.[2] That arrangement seemed to be logical, to meet with the approval of all concerned, and apparently everyone was anxious to have the Assembly meet, thus ending the inevitable lack of organization after the gigantic March revolution. "Law and order" in a way still existed and the largest part of the army was still in a state of discipline. To our great regret the meeting of the Constituent Assembly was postponed; it continued to be postponed, and it has not met yet. Some hidden power is preventing that meeting and that power is an enemy to Russia. I wish I really *knew* the Russian agent of that power! It is, of course, anarchistic but is it also traitorous and acting for the Hun?

There is another responsibility to be located, and that is the one which began the disintegration of the Army. The first official order in this connection was issued by the Ministry of the Provisional Government, possibly to gain the friendship and backing of the soldiers, so the responsibility for that must be accepted by that Ministry, but it was soon evident there would be no army under its provisions, which, in general terms, *abolished discipline*; futile efforts were made to revoke portions of it. Who prevented the restoration of discipline? I am almost persuaded it was Mr. Kerensky, who has certainly been working to gain control, and who has already become very prom-

---

[2] In the wake of Nicholas II's abdication of the throne in February 1917, all the political parties in Russia expressed a desire for a Constituent Assembly. Elections for this assembly were not held until November, however, by which time the Bolsheviks had staged their coup.

inent and popular. He dashes busily around, from rear to front and from one front to another, making impassioned speeches, but disintegration goes on and he really does nothing but make speeches! Of course it will require strength, both of *character* and in *force*, to remove any "privileges" the soldiers are enjoying, but it also requires both of those to hang a man in the United States who has committed a murder. In other words, I see so much weakness and so little strength! I have seen dead horses in the streets and the blood of killed and wounded men; I hope I will never see dead and wounded men lying in the streets. The marvelous speed with which the killed and wounded are removed from the scenes of combat still remains! This shows an ability to organize much beyond that shown in other important matters.

Cossacks from the front have arrived in Petrograd as well as other forces showing signs of active campaigning, but though the Provisional Government states it has complete control, Petrograd is practically surrounded by armed anarchists. My Russian friends assure me matters will become "normal" (normally unsettled) for a time—that the anarchists will not make another serious attempt until they have completed their organization, that they now know how easy it is to take the city and the next time they capture it they will keep it. They know their Russia and I believe them.

A Russian officer friend who came to warn us of the last uprising called recently with an automobile and took us to a beautiful place about fifteen miles in the country to call on his friends who owned the estate. We so enjoyed wandering about the large and handsome park and through the gardens. The residence is a veritable museum and one would be obliged to stay there a long time to fully appreciate and enjoy its wonders in art and antiquity. The host has about twenty officers as guests, many of whom have been wounded in the war, and I noticed that they were all well-armed; I suspect it will be unhealthy for anyone to try looting and destroying that estate! We greatly enjoyed an afternoon and evening of exquisite Russian hospitality and friendliness, which reminds me so of our own substantial Southern homes. Indeed, there is much in this Russia just now that brings to mind what I have heard of our South immediately after the Civil War.

Quite late at night we started for Petrograd and were flying along a good road near the city when we were brought to a sudden stop by a group of armed men who were quite too careless about the directions in which they pointed their firearms. Our Russian Colonel friend was in grave danger from these anarchists and he knew it, but I watched him closely and one would have thought he was bargaining for a pound of potatoes rather than for his life! For some unknown reason I was again not nervous, but was impressed with the idea I must make those people *smile*! They let us go after showing that they could hold us if they wished. My recent hostess had given me an armful of beautiful roses from her garden; while we were held, I extended them toward the group on my side of the car and finally did succeed in getting the smile for which I was trying! We were held up twice after that by Government troops and after it was all over Walter expressed himself forcibly in explaining how very like revolutions he has seen in other countries this particular experience was! However, this is a much larger and more serious situation. The suburbs of Petrograd are certainly full of armed Leninites and we are sure to hear from them again.

The Ministry has changed very considerably and Mr. Kerensky is still more prominent. He seems to do all that is done. Firing in the streets has continued but we are becoming accustomed to it. The entire city is an armed camp, but probably a very few real soldiers could very quickly take charge. How I wish they were here! The Winter Palace Square contains many men, horses, guns, motor trucks and armored cars, all presenting a very military appearance but we know how very unreliable all these men are now, and the show of force does not impress me. We continue our walks about the city, by day and by night and learn much of conditions in that way.

Worse news arrives from the Russian fronts; they are "fronts" in name only; the Russian soldiers are leaving them by the thousands; Germany and Austria are taking away many divisions. I am so sorry our Consul, Mr. Winship, is to leave us soon; he goes to Italy and while I am glad for his sake, he will be missed here. He is having many farewell dinners and luncheons given him, for he is deservedly popular. One Petrograd paper printed a positive statement that Lenin is working for Germany and is receiving German money. Whether or not he knows it, he is certainly working for Germany!

The "meetings" (Russians use this English word because, never having been allowed to "meet," they had no word for the act) on street corners have been prohibited. This removes one object of interest and also a means of obtaining information.

At last the faithful Cossacks are beginning to grumble and to make known their dissatisfaction with the Government. It is only a question of time when some of them will be contaminated by the anarchistic disease. I believe they have reason to grumble, for some of their comrades were killed in putting down the recent anarchistic revolution, yet they see that the Government takes no real steps against the revolutionists. Some were arrested but have been released. It may be fear that prevents their punishment or it may be traitors are still helping Germany to the ruination of Russia.

All is not yet lost in Russia but it will be unless strong men take charge. Where are the strong men? A small force of the Allies here now could work wonders; they will have to be sent eventually, for Europe cannot afford either of the two things now possible—first—for Germany to get complete control of Russia and—second—for Russia to become a foul nest of contagious disease, not to mention famine and other physical ills that will accompany my "second"! Of course Germany will be defeated in this war, by the Allies, in spite of Russia's failure, but it will take more time and cost more in lives and wealth than it would with Russia *still in*; if our Allies around the peace table are not more clever than the Huns, the menace of another World War remains, with the enormous resources of Russia available for Germany. It is all so clear to us I cannot understand why serious steps are not taken to prevent the *total* loss of Russia. Our excellent Red Cross and Y. M. C. A. representatives are all very well, and would be invaluable assets if working in harmony with *an armed force*, but "free Russians" will yield to nothing less than force.[3]

When I use the word "force" I certainly do not mean that Russians should be returned to serfdom; I mean the same force that is applied in all our own cities to regulate street traffic, for example. The Russian mob is a menace to civilization, in the same way that a horse, a motor car or a street car running wild in Fifth Avenue would menace the others on that street. What sane person would wish the police of New York City abolished? Here is a city, about half the size of New York, without police protection. Do not let misleading magazine articles convince you the Red Guard is a police force! One of my dearest Russian friends, Walter's interpreter, expressed the situation in words upon which I cannot improve:—"The White Guard was organized to protect the citizens from being robbed and murdered; the Red Guard was organized to rob and murder them!" These definitions are as good as any I can give; after three months of intelligent observation.

There is another expression in current use by the "Bourjewie"—or, rather, a name applied to my aversions, the "Soldiers' and Workmen's Deputies." My Russian friends make it much easier by calling them "Dog's Deputies"! That title appears in the newspapers at times, also. Speaking of the press—a most annoying article has appeared in print to the effect that Vice-Admiral Kolchak is going to the United States to assume command of the American Navy! The worst feature is that Russians believe it, though at Walter's request the Ambassador and Admiral Kolchak published denials of the story. Many Russian naval officers flocked to Walter's office for permission to accompany Admiral Kolchak!

Some of our Russian friends have let us know that they are organizing for a real counter-revolution. The fact they told us convinces us they will tell others; they only have to tell a few to prevent the success of such a revolution, for members of the old secret police are now working for the Provisional Government and such "murder will out," in Russia. I find that, while Russians intrigue excellently, only a few of them can avoid telling of it.

During the recent street fighting I decided that one was about as safe one place as another. It cannot be known when or where firing will begin; all of this adds to the excitement but is annoying. I have determined upon a new definition of optimism in Russia:—"An optimist is an alleged diplomat who is willfully blind."

---

[3] The Red Cross Mission to Russia was an effort by a group of American doctors to bring medical supplies and aid to the Russian army, initiated in 1917. It also imported cans of condensed milk to be distributed for children. Though its efforts were primarily humanitarian in nature, the Red Cross Mission was not neutral and its leaders understood that their goal was to support the Russian forces. The YMCA had established a presence in St. Petersburg in 1900; the YWCA arrived in 1917. In all three cases, the organizations engaged in an array of activities during the period of the war and the revolution in Russia.

The Embassy is now trying to obtain a supply of food from New York and I hope we can get it. It will be rather expensive by the time it reaches my table, but by that time food at *any* price will be cheap. What we get here now costs one dollar per pound; some items more, some less, but I believe that to be the average. One of my American friends here puts it higher, so I believe I am not exaggerating. A recent case of anti-American propaganda has come out; our railroad engineers have improved the traffic on some lines greatly and are now planning to assemble rolling stock at Vladivostok in crates and add it to that now in use. The cry has been started by the anarchists: "See how these American workmen take the bread out of our mouths!" And, as before, many believe it.

The correct answer is that Russian workmen, being free, won't work, and that the Americans, by putting more locomotives and cars on the roads, will increase the chances for Russians to get food by just that much more transportation. Travelling under present conditions is costly to be sure, but it is a startling experience, and one does not get wonderful experiences without venturing, so we gamble and gambol along, wishing daily both of our boys were with us.

This letter is too long—but my excuse is there is so much to tell you. I hope all of you are together on the Massachusetts coast and that Uncle Jacques is as spry as when he tried to walk me down in New York! Much love to you all.

Affectionately,

Chapter V
AFTER THE REVOLUTION[1]

Kirochnaya, 8,
Petrograd,
August 2, 1917.

My dear—

We have had a great variety of weather, politics, rumors, functions and food since I last wrote you. I accumulated *fifty eggs*, which accounts for the variety of food.

The most important and impressive function was the "Cossack Funeral," on Saturday, July 28th. I wish I had words to fully describe it! I witnessed the procession from the windows of our Consulate, on the Nevsky, but Walter went to St. Isaac's Cathedral, and drove with the Ambassador to various places along the route. The square, surrounded by the Cathedral, Astoria and English Hotels, Marinsky Palace and the ex-German Embassy, was packed with humanity and lined with representatives from many regiments, also many sailors, all under arms and accompanied by bands. In addition a great many armed soldiers were stationed all over the city, and particularly along the line of march of the procession, to preserve order. These soldiers were particularly keen to see that all windows along the route were closed, it being a habit in this country, as said, to shoot into a crowd from windows.

This procession was unique in that it carried no red banners—the first one have seen since I arrived that was free from them. High officials, military, clergy, men, women and children all took part. The dirges by the numerous bands were effectively appropriate and reminded one of great *waves* of music. The whole funeral reflects credit upon those who arranged it and who stated positively beforehand there must be no demonstrations, no disorders, and there were none. Once again we are convinced these people *can* do right if they will!

The floral offerings were wonderful in beauty and number; many were carried by those marching, and the caskets of the dead were almost hidden by them. The riderless horses of the dead Cossacks following each coffin added to the solemnity while the magnificent singing by the marching priests and boys must be heard to be appreciated. It was interesting to see the stern faces of the Cossacks who were riding in the procession. Their expressions seemed to say:—"We have lost some of our comrades

---

[1] Crosley entitled this section "After the Revolution," but at this point in her letters the "real" revolution, that of the Bosheviks, is yet to come.

in the fight to put down the revolution—after the next fight in which we take part the heavier losses will be on the other side!"

One day a party of eight, Walter being the only man, went up the Neva by steamer to Lake Ladoga,[2] getting off and wandering about during the two hours the steamer remained there before leaving again for Petrograd. We saw the famous Castle (and Prison) of Schlusselberg,[3] in which have been confined some of the most renowned prisoners of Russia, including Czar Paul.[4] The river trip is well worth while and drove the cobwebs of Petrograd from our brains!

It will be interesting for you to know that I have met many of the men now prominent in Russia, including President of the Duma Rodzianko, Foreign Minister Terestchenko and Professor Miliukov.

The rumors are infinitely large and varied. All Russians anticipate bloodshed in the near future and also in large amounts. There seems really to be no necessity for such an upheaval as our Russian friends assure me will take place, for if the patriotic people would ORGANIZE, *organize*, they could do wonders! They insist that they cannot organize, and I suppose they should know. I was told by a relative of Mr. Guchkov that he, Kerensky, Kornilov,[5] Brusilov,[6] and others are in frequent consultation for the purpose of deciding upon the form of a new government, but, while they *talk* Lenin is drilling his men!

I had thought the bread lines were as long as possible before, but as we walk about at night now we find them growing daily. Speaking of "lines" and the variety that

---

[2] Lake Ladoga is a freshwater lake about twenty-five miles east of St. Petersburg. During World War II, when Leningrad (St. Petersburg) was under siege by the German army, Lake Ladoga became the "Road of Life" that allowed food and supplies to be brought into the city.

[3] Schlusselberg was a fourteenth-century fortress near St. Petersburg converted to a prison by Peter the Great. Over the next two centuries, it held a number of well-known political prisoners, such as participants in the Decembrist uprising and Lenin's brother, who was hanged for treason in 1887.

[4] Paul I was the son of Catherine II (the Great) and ruled Russia from 1796 to 1801, when he was murdered by a group of conspirators who wanted to place his son Alexander I on the throne.

[5] General Lavr G. Kornilov (1870–1918) was a decorated soldier who had served with distinction in the Russo-Japanese War and later led several armies on the Western Front in the first years of World War I. After the fall of the monarchy in February 1917, Kornilov had disagreements with the Provisional Government; in August, after being accused of plotting a coup d'etat, he proceeded to do just that, and was arrested. He escaped from custody during the October Revolution and eventually joined the "Whites," who fought against Bolshevik control over the next three years. He was killed in action in 1918.

[6] Aleksei A. Brusilov (1853–1926) was a Russian general in the Imperial Army. He is most known for his offensive tactics. The last successful Russian offensive of World War I, known as the Brusilov Offensive, occurred in March 1916. Brusilov died of natural causes in 1926.

exists, I saw a new one! Bread lines, meat lines, milk lines, playing card (soldiers only), tobacco lines, shoe lines, etc., are common, but to day there were several Russians in line waiting to give money to a beggar! (Russians have a superstition about giving to beggars.)

An interesting cable has arrived from Washington and a similar one from London, to the effect that the anarchists here are going to arrange the murder of all Allied Attaches. While we do not believe it and no one has changed his habits because of it, this bears out my statement about the variety of rumors again. Also, I might add, it does not increase my peace of mind. Petrograd remains an armed camp, and, there being apparently no use for armored cars at the other fronts, many have come to the "Petrograd front" and are dashing madly about the city, their shrill sirens adding to the other nerve-racking noises, but their presence adding to the scenery!

I found another example of anti-American propaganda, a translation of which I will copy here, for it covers much ground and will show what sorts of arguments are used and believed.

TRANSLATION OF AN ARTICLE IN A FINNISH NEWSPAPER (Wilborg)
"In America"

The American Capital is restless. That is well known. If the Russian workmen, if all the Democracy of Russia knew what "Liberty and Freedom" of America really is, they would wish to have nothing in common with that America; on the contrary they would fight against it with more ardor; against the imperialistic bandits who enrich themselves at the expense of unfortunate Russia.

We have already had a visit from an American delegation (that of Root), which apparently comes to aid democratic Russia, but, in fact, came to occupy itself with imperialistic intrigue, for financial transactions, and ended by giving a secret ultimatum to the Provisional Government, an ultimatum which has had a decisive influence on the politics of the coalition and of the offensive. Soon another delegation came to Russia. What for?

In that country (United States) "truly democratic," it is not rare that the striking workmen are shot, without sparing even the children nor the aged. Their houses are even burned. There are shot even the political strugglers and they are also imprisoned, or condemned to hard labor.

When the American Capitalists had exacted of their government a declaration of war against Germany, the people protested and demanded a referendum, but the "truly democratic" Wilson replied with a categorical refusal, declaring that the demand was made through the instigation of German spies. Wilson knew very well that his bloody project would "fall into the water" if the democracy was consulted. In spite of the protestations of the workmen the war was declared, to the very great happiness of the bankers and the manufacturers of munitions. In America they have introduced compulsory military service, creating that militarism against which they claim they are fighting.

No! The Russian workmen cannot and must not believe these agents of American Capital, agents sent to Russia to exploit us under the same conditions that they exploit the population of America!

This fable shows how easy it is, for those so inclined, to twist honest efforts to suit their own dishonest ends. It would be easy to answer the many articles like the one quoted above, but to do it effectively would require a large force and much money, for a reply, to be efficient, must appear immediately such articles are seen, and efforts must be made to get the reply to the same places the original articles go. Unless one reads the reply he will believe the original. But for the seriousness of the matter one could laugh, but the Russians *believe* what they read, and hundreds now believe in the truth of that article about our "Capitalists."

Two excellent examples of the readiness with which educated Russians believe statements that cannot be true have recently come to my attention. A committee of Russian Naval Officers called upon Walter with the request that the large number (one hundred) of officers they represented be permitted to go on board the American battleship then at Revel which had come there for the purpose of receiving such Russian officers as might wish to serve in the American Navy! Though they were naval officers they did not appreciate the utter impossibility for a hostile battleship to enter the Baltic, past the German defenses! Another committee representing two hundred Polish officers in the Russian Navy called and reported: "In view of the fact you are now manning ships of the American Navy entirely with Poles, we wish to go and offer our services to officer those ships for you because so few of your officers speak our language!" In both those cases Walter had great difficulty in convincing the committees that what they believed to be true could not be, and it all shows what rich ground for propaganda is furnished by the Russian minds. The Germans know all about this. Are they neglecting the wonderful opportunity? Are we? Many believe the Germans will come to Petrograd with an army, but I do not. Why should they undertake such a military effort? The Russians (also paid agents) are doing better work for Germany than a German army could do.

I am still studying hard at my Russian lessons. I must quit to study now. With much love to you all.

From,

Kirochnaya, 8,
Petrograd,
August 9, 1917.

My dear—

Nothing very important has occurred during the last week! (We learn to consider the words "important" and "serious" as having about the same meaning!) Wild rumors continue—some are confirmed and some are not. Frequent meetings and consultations are held by those interested in the good of Russia and many plans discussed, but every plan requires *money*! We read of the fabulous sums being appropriated, subscribed and spent, but there does not seem to be any available for work in Russia. Discouraging!

A Russian friend who enjoys shooting gave me a most acceptable present of two large birds he had shot. They furnished a most satisfactory addition to our limited diet.

We have observed the American flag being used by Russians as a means of protection. This argues that our flag is now considered by them as least likely to be molested, and accounts for more anti-American propaganda that is being spread about. We read of agitation in the States to prevent the draft law from being passed; the most prominent name we see in print in this connection is that of Emma Goldman, and is it only a coincidence that we see published in Russia at about the same time a long letter purporting to be signed by Emma Goldman and Alexander Berkman,[7] and addressed to "Russian Brothers, Comrades, Workmen"?

This letter states that the Mooneys, Weinberg, Newland, and Billings,[8] all comrades, working for the same revolutionary cause, are "threatened by the gallows" and that "we really were in great difficulties to help them"! It also warns Russians not to believe that the United States is fighting for democracy and liberty, citing the excellent manner in which our authorities have subdued strike riots as proving that we cannot be fighting for "liberty and humanity"! "We will fight to our last breath

---

[7] Emma Goldman (1869–1940) was born in the Russian Empire and later emigrated to the United States, where she became an anarchist, political activist, and writer. Alexander Berkman (1870–1936) was a Lithuanian immigrant and anarchist leader in the United States. Goldman and Berkman attempted to assassinate the American industrialist Henry Frick. Both were imprisoned several times for their activities. Berkman committed suicide in 1936; Goldman died after suffering several strokes.

[8] Crosley is referring to the 1917 trial of labor leader Thomas Mooney (1882–1942), convicted of the San Francisco Preparedness Bombing of 1916, for throwing a bomb during a parade to acknowledge the United States' eventual entry into World War I. Warren K. Billings (1893–1972) was a labor leader and political activist who was also convicted for this bombing and served twenty-three years in prison. Israel Weinberg was also put on trial with the bombing, but was acquitted. Crosley has mistakenly referred to a "Newland" involved in the same affair; it was actually Edward Nolan.

against the American plutocracy" is a message well calculated to please and inflame the ones here who seek to abolish law and order.

"And you, dear friends, on your behalf, do all you possibly can to attain results of the great ideas of anarchism" is advice that one might expect from people employed by our Hun enemies, and is a confirmation of my belief that *anarchy* is what they are after. The ending of the letter is particularly inspiring to soldiers who won't fight and to work men who won't work: "Down with the Government and the War!" "Down with Capitalism!" "Hurrah for the Social Revolution!" "Hurrah for Anarchism!" All these appeared in the letter and they seem to omit nothing in the way of *de*struction; I fail to find anything in the letter advising *con*struction!

Speaking of workmen who won't work, a rather amusing thing happened at a "street corner meeting" and was witnessed by a friend who told me of it. A Russian student with a sense of wit and also with an apparent disregard for consequences began addressing a crowd of workmen:—"You are workmen! The world cannot advance without you!" *Cheers!* "You are workmen! The world needs you!" *More cheers!* "You are workmen! You are in the majority!" *Many more cheers!* "You are workmen! Your labor is a noble thing!" *Wild cheering!* "You are workmen! *Therefore you should work!*" *Howls of rage*, and an attempt to overtake the student who, at the end of his last remark ran away, laughing merrily!

The weather has changed from a variety to perpetual intense heat but we get some relief at night. Also, we get smoke from burning forests, at times quite dense. We hear constant reports of the destruction of beautiful and valuable forests by the peasants, who apparently have no reason for burning except to "spite" the owners!

Constant efforts are being made to form a "Government" but the result is that anything resembling a *government* is rapidly disappearing. My abominations, "The Soldiers' and Workmen's Deputies," are becoming more insistent and more powerful; their final seat in the saddle seems more certain each day, but it will be a sad day for the poor horse when they are firmly seated. The many groups of soldiers all over the city remain very much in evidence, but one is impressed with the belief that it would require very few *real* soldiers to overpower them readily. The individual members of these groups feel at times that they must do their duty, and, as we walk about on our information gathering exercise, we are frequently stopped and questioned. The sentries do not know why they stop us nor what they want to ask us, and we are always permitted to pass after assuming an interrogative attitude of our own! It would be highly amusing if there were not so much at stake.

We have had a most interesting and instructive visit to Tsarskoe Selo and to Pavlosk. We took the dear little interpreter and it was both pitiful and impressive to see the respect shown her by the old retainers at Tsarskoe Selo. They all recognized her and her presence permitted us to see many things and places we could not have seen without her. She showed us the home her family had always occupied—were occupying when the revolution took place. Her bravery is inspiring to see. The

Czar's church, though small, is a beautiful gem and is filled with a priceless collection of Ikons and embroideries, representing gifts from all parts of Russia. One could spend weeks studying them. Another touching situation was shown by the numbers of questions asked Miss Guerardy by the old retainers. "When will the Czar return to power?" "How soon will we be free of these monsters?" "Will you be living in your own house again soon?" At Pavlosk we enjoyed the parks, and, above all, the wonderful native Russian orchestra! I am now certain that this music appeals to me more than any other. I believe it to be superior to the old Hungarian music which has always been my favorite.

The Ambassador gave a reception for our departing Consul, and the members of the American Red Cross Mission to Russia, who arrived last night, were among the guests. They are very interesting men and there is much for them to do in Russia. How I wish some real Government, or force, could be behind them here! I'm not pessimistic, but we can see the difficulties ahead of them so clearly! They will propose and the "Dogs' Deputies" will dispose.

There have been a number of social gatherings, dinners, luncheons, teas—some at our home—but the times are too strenuous for real pleasure. Without these modest opportunities for friends to get together it would be very much more strenuous. Just now the wood question is critical. We are borrowing again! We never know when mail will arrive or leave, so it is very probable you will receive many of my letters at the same time, if ever.

In spite of all the difficulties and the evident demoralization it is remarkable how we continue to *hope*! The Russian character does permit a complete reversal of ideas within twenty-four hours; I know that many Russians are "plotting" to establish a good government; therefore I hope, from day to day, that their efforts will have a beneficial result. It is *possible* only, for their handicaps are enormous. "Made in Germany" may, I believe, be applied to the shoddy government here, as well as to shoddy manufactured products I have seen here and elsewhere.

It is even possible that the soldiers who are now murdering their officers and running away from the Germans might again become good soldiers, for no one can deny that they fought bravely for many months. However, when one hears of the horrible crimes these same soldiers are now committing against their own people during their cowardly retreats, it requires philosophy to continue to hope. In the various literature and speeches intended to incite the soldiers the words "freedom," "annexations," "contributions," "representation," "propaganda" are often used. Probably only an exceedingly small per cent of the soldiers know the meaning of any of these words. They do not originate them. Who does?

To many of us here it seems that a Japanese army should be on the road to the Russian fronts. It is so obvious to us that I am certain it won't happen early enough to be of real value. I find it is the obvious thing to retain Russia with us, which is not done.

It makes me almost peevish to learn of the attractive living conditions once existing here, and to compare them with our present lack of mental and physical comfort! A ray of hope concerning a supply of wood just intruded! That doubt and fact has been one of our greatest discomforts, but a contractor has promised to deliver a large consignment from Finland to the Embassy. The cost of what we have asked for will be five hundred dollars, which, for heating an apartment about five months, might be considered expensive! No necessity is deemed expensive here *if we can get it*.

The so-called socialists are having a free hand here to try out their pet theories, and, as their efforts cost me much money and discomfort, I cannot subscribe to them. I consider the "Socialists" a failure here, as they must be in any country unless they are able to modify the *results* of their theories! When I can see *con*struction I may believe, but not sooner.

I estimate that the Commission headed by Mr. Root is with you about now, and we are hoping great hopes that the people of the United States will be told of the conditions existing here when the Commission left, though even that will not tell them what exists now, as said conditions grow worse daily. The Commission even missed the July revolution—the anarchists being too well-advised to start it while the Commission remained in Petrograd.

I hope you have received my letters, but I have no assurance that you have. What a blessing a good mail service is, and how I long for one! But these are war days! Always with love to all.

Yours,

Kirochnaya, 8,
Petrograd,
Sunday, August 19, 1917.

My dear—

There is still a dearth of exciting news, though a great deal happens. Details would bore you for they would sound so alike in each letter I write you; therefore I will again generalize by saying that everything here grows steadily worse. By that statement I mean that Russia is no longer in "our war" and cannot be brought back in it. And when I consider what that means to the United States and our Allies, the lack of food and other physical comforts fades into insignificance, and the Russian-Army Rearward-Marathon is the most important thing in the whole world!

More details of the horrible crimes committed by the fleeing soldiers continue to be given me by the wives of Russian officers who have escaped with their lives from the fast melting fronts and they are too terrible to put into print. Use your imagination; try to remember everything unpleasant of which you have ever heard as happening to human beings; those, and more, are happening to Russians, but the saddest part of it all is that the crimes are being committed by Russians! Yet we are told that these men can govern! I have yet to hear of a court of justice punishing a criminal, though of course many punishments, including death, have been assigned without trial; think of it!

We have been again to the beautiful estate of Colonel Vsevolosky, near Petrograd. There was a large party for the weekend, and where the terrible conditions in Russia were temporarily ignored, a very pleasant gathering. Walter had some excellent ptarmigan shooting, and, in addition, some much-needed exercise, of which he gets too little. The visit further impressed me with the pitiful situation in which nice Russians now find themselves. The guard of officer friends remains at this beautiful place but their number is too small to keep off a large force. Such a force may arrive at any time, yet the bravery of these good people permits them to act as though nothing threatens; how I wish I could help them!

Heretofore the St. George Cross was a decoration given only for military service of the highest character, so you can imagine that the wearers of it would form a body of rather superior persons. Some of our friends are members of the St. George Society[9] and, through them, we have met many other members. I am told that the Cross has more recently been awarded for no service whatever, this furnishing another example of destruction.

Small social affairs continue and my days at home are becoming most interesting "functions." Friends bring their friends and my circle is enlarging rapidly. We brought a supply of sugar and tea with us so I shall not run short of them, but it is a problem to find something more substantial to serve. The drinking water is also a problem! One cannot drink the city water in safety because it is taken from the Neva where it is an open sewer. Bottled water is becoming very difficult to obtain and is unreliable when found. To boil and filter the city water is beyond the comprehension of a Russian cook —so we are obliged to attend to that detail ourselves, as are many other housekeepers.

We hear that the Germans have decided to occupy Riga; the word "capture" hardly applies, for when they want it seriously the "Red" Russians will run away! I fancy the Huns will be more comfortable in Riga next winter than in the trenches outside.

Today we went to a solemn service at St. Isaac's Cathedral; I would like to describe that singing for you but words fail me. I would not have missed the music I have heard in Russia for a great deal; it appeals to me more than ever.

News from Ukraine is bad; more secession, with a little government and army of their own; fights between Ukrainian "army" and Russian soldiers; ultimatum from Ukraine to Petrograd to immediately remove all Russian soldiers from her bound-

---

[9] The Royal Society of St. George is an English patriotic and social society that engages in social aid.

aries; Huns waiting to march in and pick up spoils of provisions! It is all so sickening when one realizes the benefits the Germans are getting from the Russian turmoil!

One member of the Root Commission stated in my hearing before he left for the United States "there is plenty of food in Russia"! If you hear that statement you may deny it in my name. There is plenty of food here for a *large* flock of canary birds; there is even enough for the army; there is enough for the civilian population, but there is not enough for all three of those. I form a part of the civilian population, do marketing, and *I know*. So many of our friends here have lost weight since we arrived; our arrival is not the cause of the loss of weight, but there is nearly every other reason why one should lose weight here!

The ex-Czar and his unhappy family have been removed from Tsarskoe Selo and taken to—where? We cannot learn. There was considerable talk of an escape or a rescue, and it is generally believed that Mr. Kerensky, who seems to be the only "Ministry" Russia has now, decided to remove them all to a "safer" place. In my opinion there is no safe place in Russia for the ex-Royal Family.

My friends are very complimentary about my success with this very difficult language, and I really surprise myself at times with my ability to understand and make myself understood. Its study certainly furnishes one with a never-failing occupation, which, in itself, is a very good thing to have at this particular time!

Now we know that the Root Commission has reached Washington as do our Russian friends, and that knowledge on their part is a source of frequent embarrassment to us. They ask: "Why did your Root Commission come to Russia?" "The Root Commission did a great deal of talking here and made many promises; they are in Washington now, but where is the help they promised?" "Why does the rich United States help all her other Allies so wonderfully and do nothing for Russia?" As I cannot answer any of those questions to my own satisfaction I am obliged to "beat around the bush" considerably when my Russian friends ask them!

Russia is a wonderful land and one which offers all kinds of opportunities to American businessmen. That is, if and when law and order are established, citizens of the United States could reap harvests of legitimate wealth here if armed with the good will of the people. That good will existed in a marked degree not long ago. It is being driven away by our enemies, who, with a different object, ask the Russian "proletariat" the same questions my friends ask me. Of course I appreciate how difficult it is for anyone so far away as you are to realize just what is needed here—but! I am sure you *can* realize that those here charged with the duty of knowing certainly do know more than you do! That simple problem of "*Why?*" is the hardest one for us to solve.

Since I began this letter I have had some callers and one related to me the report of a Russian officer who had been at Tarnopol[10] when the Russians beat such a

---

[10] This rout in July 1917 was known as the Kerensky Offensive and was the last Russian offensive of the war.

disgraceful retreat from the German advance. This officer reports that the Germans took moving pictures of the Russians engaged in the most terrible excesses against their own people, and that the Russian soldiers committed much worse crimes against their fellow citizens than the Germans did in 1914 in Belgium! Isn't it a horrible mess? I have read much Russian history since my arrival here and it is really remarkable how it is repeating what has happened from time to time since there began to be a Russia.

We hear of some excellent work done in Vladivostok by the men on liberty from the U.S.S. *Buffalo*! It is reported here that they refused to meet or to have anything to do with the Russian sailors there, on the grounds that the Russians were mutinous and approved of the actions of their fellows who murdered their officers! That is reported to have made a great impression on the Russian sailors in Vladivostok and it has even done some good here. Just think how that effect could be multiplied by a comparatively small force of *armed* American troops! There are *so many efforts* that *could* be made! It is the total absence of effort that makes one wonder to a headache!

Our mail communication grows worse. I have just received replies to letters written nearly four months ago. I have no means of knowing how our plan to pass these letters around is working, but you will readily realize that I cannot write letters of this size to many people! Please, all of you, send us newspaper clippings—it is easier than sending the papers and will give us a great variety of news, of which we need all we can get. I never before realized the value of "news from home"—I suppose because it was never so difficult to obtain!

The activities of the women soldiers increase, but their successes do not. Their original intention to shame the men soldiers has failed utterly. We hear remarkable stories of Cossacks being placed on guard to protect the women soldiers from the remainder of the Russian army!

The big question here is: "Will the Germans take Petrograd?" They can take it at any time, but I still believe they will not make the effort. Everything here is going fine for the Germans, so there is no good reason for them to send an army here. They will take Riga and as much of the surrounding country as they need to make themselves snug for the winter, but I cannot believe they will come here now, though I am not alone in being unable to decide what the German General Staff plans to do!

Now I must attend to important housekeeping; routine goes on in the home even if all outside in Russia is upset. Much love to all of you from both of us.

Affectionately yours,

Kirochnaya, Vosyem,
Petrograd,
August 28, 1917.

My dear Son:

We are moving and this is the last letter you will receive from this address, though fortunately we do not change our *number*! That is to say, our friends, Mr. and Mrs. Smith, have left for the States and we will take their apartment very soon. We are taking small packages there and are packing our few belongings. Social affairs now consist almost entirely in entertaining among foreigners, and it is wrong, for no one needs cheering more than our Russian friends. When we get into our new apartment, which lends itself better to entertaining, I will do more than I have been able to do here.

Our friend, Colonel Vsevolosky, brought me a large number of beautiful flowers from his handsome gardens, and they help this apartment very much. As with other things pertaining to the "Bourjewie," the cultivation and use of flowers is not what it once was here.

We are now able to get some items of provisions from the Embassy though the supply elsewhere is more limited than ever. Recently, while walking in one of the parks in the evening, we saw an American flag flying; upon reaching it we found a large sign which read (in Russian) "American Auction," and there was an auction such as I have not seen before going on. Each person *paid* what he bid, in the hope that no one would bid (and pay) a larger sum! You can readily see how one really anxious to purchase an article would have to pay dearly if someone outbid him a few times! It was very interesting to watch, but very suddenly those in charge seemed to observe our interest in the flag, whereupon it was hastily folded up and hurried away! Surely this is a strange country!

We continue our long walks and derive continued knowledge and exercise from them. We also study Russian while out for a walk, reading signs and *posters*. "Freedom" has been interpreted to mean that anyone may put a glaring poster in any place, and walls, fences and columns once sacred are now freely papered, including those of the Winter Palace and other public buildings, thereby detracting considerably from their appearance, but giving us a Russian lesson.

It is interesting to note the gradual disappearance of the thousands of red flags so much in evidence when we arrived here; do not think for a moment this argues for a change of sentiment! It only means that the weather has frayed and faded the flags, and the supply of red material is not equal to the demand. There are still plenty of red banners for the many processions, the inscriptions thereupon being designed to terrorize those who wear clean clothes, but mostly the "Bourjewie" and the "Capitalists" are the targets at which they aim in savage terms. I have not discovered in which class they put me, but discreetly cover any article of dress that *might* rouse their ire with something almost shabby when I go on the street. *Think* of a country, a Capital, in which it is unwise to appear on the street "well dressed"! I suppose the war has made a difference in most countries, but it is a fact I have not seen a man wearing a silk hat in this large Capital of a large country!

No one knows how despondent, how desperate, all better classes of Russians are, to say nothing of the humiliation and weariness they suffer. The agonies of war for three years were bad enough and now that the additional troubles have come their life is a staggering problem. A smattering of religion remains, but when the Russians lost their Czar they really lost their church. Some are still devout and cross themselves when passing a church or an Ikon, but the number of those who do it is noticeably decreasing. I believe the good ones miss their Czar and their church. The so-called "Bolsheviks" are here with destructive desire and force; one cannot reason with them; they are just impossible tempest breeders, real agitators like the disturbing elements in our own large cities.

I feel sure the most of our trouble-makers come from here; their faces look so much like these I see here among the masses. (Of course I do not refer to the well-known German-made brand of troubles we have recently had at home, though these people would make willing and able agents of the Germans.)

I have heard from one of my excellent sources of information that the ex-Czar who we now know is in Tobolsk with his family said: "I do not grieve for myself, but for my people and all the trouble I brought upon them!" He was undoubtedly weak, and he certainly exercised bad judgment, but I believe he was a good man.

We are promised another revolution next week, which leads me to believe we will not get it at that time. All schedules in Russia are "off"! We will, of course, have other revolutions, but we will *not* have a week of warning. Russian Red revolutionists are like other bullies; they do not accurately carry out their threats—though there is a remarkable exception to that general rule visible here. There will be published in the papers a most extraordinary "promise" of a decree or ruling to be put into effect, and we all say: "But that is impossible—it *can't* be done!" But it is done, and no one rebels. There is a rumor that the Russian soldiers have stopped running away from their fat German brothers because said brothers are out of breath through chasing the Russians. If this be true who can say they are without compassion!

The Moscow Convention has the stage; this Convention has been much advertised as being the one thing that would fix up Russia for all time; as a matter of fact much will be said there, while little will be done. Russia's best men can make wonderful speeches—that ability is not confined to the "best" men—but *organize*? Apparently not!

Recently a Russian sent us four delicious ducks he had shot; they were accompanied by an invitation to your father to go and shoot some. I hope he can go, for he will get exercise and recreation whether or not he gets ducks. We had another attractive invitation to go to the country where your father was to shoot quail, but bad weather, an explosion in an ammunition factory, a broken telephone connection and a disabled automobile all worked together to prevent our departure as planned. We really needed the quail, too! You see there are many difficulties hereabouts.

It seems ages since we heard from you! We learn some mail will arrive tomorrow night and news from you will be very welcome. As other living conditions grow worse mail from home becomes more precious.

General Kornilov, a Cossack, has been made Commander-in-Chief of the Armies, and from all I can learn, if anyone can bring order out of chaos, he can do it. Your father knows General K. and admires him very much. It was *rumored* recently that Mr. Kerensky, for personal selfish reasons, would remove General Kornilov from his high command; that the Cossacks heard of the intention and issued an ultimatum to the effect that their General Kornilov is the best man for the place and that he *must* remain Commander-in-Chief! He still remains, but not for long, because no one stays long in high places in Russia these days! A semblance of a General Staff is retained in Petrograd, but one of the staff officers recently told my best Russian friend he could not learn just where the armies are; they have run so far and so fast they can't be located!

Facts about the much-boasted "offensive" staged for the Root Commission are beginning to leak out and into Petrograd, and many are accordingly sad. It seems that the Russian force which advanced against the Germans while being observed by members of the Commission was composed largely of volunteer officers and that a very great number of them were killed—some being friends and relatives of my friends, so I am forced to believe the truth is as stated by them. All this, coupled with the tales of wonderful heroism during the early part of the war convinces me that there is *much of good in Russians and that someday Russia will be the wonderful, place nature seems to have intended it to be.* When I use similar expressions to the Russians they say: "Perhaps, but we will not be here to see it!"

I believe it to be a fact that Russia lost many of her best men, both officers and enlisted men, early in the war; that, since the revolution a large percentage of the remaining good officers have been murdered; I do not believe it above the possibilities that the lists of those murdered were largely prepared under orders from Berlin. Starting with a small percentage of "good" men, considering how many are dead, not many are left to reconstruct Russia.

British guns furnished the Russian Armies are now in the possession of the Germans; *given* to them by the Russians; some guns have gone direct through the lines without being unloaded from the freight cars; comparatively large supplies of food and "munitions" have come into the possession of the Huns without an effort having been necessary on their part! Isn't it a horrible mess! The Russian Navy has ceased to exist. There are some ships upon which alleged sailors live, but they are too demoralized to be considered as a Navy. In the meantime, when particularly brutal work is desired by the "Dogs' Deputies," we learn that "Kronstadt Sailors" do it.

Many members of the foreign colony are leaving Petrograd, more particularly the women, and it will be lonesome here on that account. Business men are being forced to close their factories and officers are leaving as fast as their affairs permit. When I say "lonesome" don't think I mean *dull*! The Russians will keep us guessing and probably entertained as well.

Many more of those who took part in the July revolution and were arrested have been released without punishment, and it is generally believed no punishments will be given to those who tried so hard to institute anarchy here. It looks like encouragement to me! I understand that very few of the nice Russians will return to Petrograd this Fall, but will, with thousands of others, remain in hiding and seek to avoid disaster. I have visions of these devoted people running from one place to another in Russia seeking safety! I am truly sorry for them, whatever their sins may have been—if any.

It is late, and I must leave you. I hope you have received all previous letters, including the shorter, more intimate notes. All of our love for you!

Affectionately,
Mother.

Chapter VI
RIGA CAPTURED

Franzhuskaya Nabrizhnaya, Vosyem,
Petrograd,
September 6, 1917.

My dear—:

In my last letter I mentioned the Moscow Convention and the many useless speeches that would be made there; I also mentioned General Kornilov, though I did not know he was to make a speech; he did make one, and I like it so much I am going to put it in this letter. I have read all the speeches made there, and the one by the Commander-in-Chief is not only good, but is official, and is the only one in which I have any confidence. It follows:

Moscow, August 27, 1917.

As the Commander-in-Chief I welcome the Provisional Government and the meeting thereof, in the name of the Active Armies. I would be glad if I could welcome you in the name of armies that are standing on our frontiers like a rigid wall, guarding the Russian lands, honor and dignity, but it is with great sorrow I must add and say openly that I have no assurance the Russian Army will do its duty to the country.

My telegram to the Provisional Government dated July 9 and concerning the restoration of capital punishment for traitors is well known to all. The immediate necessity for that telegram was the dishonor of the defeat at Tarnopol, and such a demoralization as Russian arms have never known. The dishonor of that defeat is the result of secret propaganda which has brought our once famous and glorious army to its present condition through outside influences and unwise methods of reorganization.

The measures taken by the Provisional Government after the receipt of my telegram certainly brought some improvement to the army, but the destructive propaganda continues, and I will give you proof of this. During the early part of August some soldiers who had ceased to be warriors murdered their own officers. The Commander of the 43rd Siberian Rifle Regiment was bayonetted by his men, but when they refused to deliver the instigators and the guilty ones, they were surrounded by another regiment and ordered by the representative of the Provisional Government to deliver them or be fired upon, the guilty regiment, with men weeping, begged for pardon, like the cowards they were! (In addition to the Commanders of the forces in the field there is an officer or a civilian called the "Commissaire," who represents the Provisional Government at that particular front. He seems to be there in the capacity of one to report upon what occurs and to give orders, just as though they came from the Provisional Government direct. He is really an additional "Commander," whole authority seems to be absolute.) The criminals were all delivered and were tried by a revolutionary court-martial; they are now awaiting sentence, which they will not fail to receive. After that the regiment promised to wipe out its dishonor. (Note—No punishment has been awarded these men at this date; it is most likely they will not be punished as such an act will not be permitted by the "Dogs' Deputies"! Many hundreds of officers have been murdered but I can learn of no punishments for their murderers.)

All these murders are accomplished by the soldiers under surroundings of a most peculiar character. A very remarkable and ugly feeling of freedom, unlimited darkness of intellect, and a most disgusting "Hooliganism" prevails among the men. Some days ago, during the German advance on Riga, the 56th Siberian Rifle Regiment left its position without orders and left behind their guns and ammunition, and it was only under threat, after I gave the order to destroy the entire regiment, that it returned to its place. Only by such vigorous measures can we fight anarchy in the Army and we will crush that anarchy, but the danger of new devastation hangs over the country; we are threatened with the loss of more territory, more towns, and the loss of the Capital itself.

The conditions at the front are such that, on account of the demoralization of the army, we have lost all of Galicia, all of Bukovino, and all of the fruits of our actual victories of the past years. In some places the enemy has crossed our frontier and is threatening our fertile provinces of the South. The enemy is trying to wipe out the Rumanian Army and to force Rumania to withdraw from the Allies. The enemy is at the doors of Riga, and if our Army is in such condition that it cannot retain its positions on the shores of the Gulf of Riga, the way to Petrograd is open. As a heritage from the old regime Free Russia received an army which had faults of organization, but it was an army that could fight; it was stoical and was ready for great self-sacrifice. Because of a great many legislative acts prepared after the revolution by persons *who were in total ignorance of the spirit of the army*, that army was transformed into an angry mob caring only for its life!

As examples of their condition whole regiments expressed a desire to make peace with Germany; were ready to give up their country, the provinces that had been captured, and even wished to collect one hundred rubles per man to pay an indemnity! The Army must be restored at any price; without an army Russia cannot be saved; without an army there will be no more "Free Russia." For the restoration of the Army the measures which I reported to the Provisional Government must be taken immediately. My report was presented and was signed, approved, without any reservations, by the Secretary of War, Savinkov, and by the Commissaire at the General Staff, Krylenko.

In a few words I will give you the principles of my report on "iron discipline": Deductions from history and from military training show there can be no army without discipline; only an army united by iron discipline, guided by the single stern will of its Commander, is capable of a victory or is worthy of one. The discipline must be confirmed in the everyday work of the army, giving a proper amount of power to the subordinate commanders, to the officers, and to the non-commissioned officers.

I will remind those who, with the best intentions, made proposals for peace, that even if a conclusion of peace were possible without great dishonor to the country, peace could not obtain now on account of the great demoralization of the troops. The disorganized flow of unrestrained released soldiers would devastate the country. It is necessary to increase the prestige of the officers. The body of officers who had fought valiantly during the war immediately declared, in great majority, for the revolution, and remained faithful to the deeds of the revolution, must be recompensed for the great humiliation that has been endured by them and the systematic abuse they have received through no fault of their own. The material position of the officers must be bettered; also of their widows, orphans and wives; and, by the way, it is just to remark that the officers are the only body in all Russia that has not spoken of its needs, and asked for an improvement in their material position! What that material position is, is best shown by the fate of the officer on the street of Petrograd, who fainted from hunger because he had no money to buy food.

I am not an enemy of the Committees of soldiers; I have worked with them as the Commander of the 8th Army, and as the Chief of the South East Front; but I request that their activities be concerned only with the household and the interior life of the army, without any interference with the strategical questions nor the choice of their leaders! I acknowledge the Commissaires as a present necessity, as a fact, but the guarantee of the efficiency of that necessity depends upon the personality of the Commissaire; he should be one in which the democratization of political views corresponds with his tact, his energy, and his ability to assume responsibilities at times very great.

Without an organized rear there can be no army. All measures taken in the Army will be fruitless sacrifices, but inevitable to the restoration of order, and the country cannot be made happy if the disciplined army remains without recruits, supplies, uniforms and ammunition. Measures taken at the front must also be taken in the rear; the guiding idea must be their expediency for the salvation of the country.

I have proof that our railroads are in such a condition that in November they will not be in a state to transport the necessities for the armies, and the armies will be without convoy. I will not enlarge upon the consequences of such a condition. I have just received a telegram from the Commander of the South East Front which I will read to you: "On the front there is flour hunger; in the shops and markets there is no flour; all the bakers are closing their shops; all the biscuits in store are, for the first time during the war, exhausted; they have been used for the reserves. I have taken all possible steps to add to the supplies; the assistance of the government is a necessity; the front cannot exist like this any longer."

The question of ammunition is not any better; in fact, the productivity of our factories working for the army has fallen to such an extent that now, in round numbers, the productivity in the principal needs of the army, when compared with the figures for the time from October, 1916, to January, 1917, has fallen sixty per cent. I can only give figures. However, if it continues in this way, *our armies will be in the same condition they were in the spring of 1915*, during what has been called our retreat from Poland, Galicia, and the Carpathians.

For the successful employment of our artillery we must have airplanes, but our position is such that we cannot replace our losses; since we cannot replace our losses in machines we cannot replace them in men, for there are no machines upon which to train them. At present the productivity of the airplane factories has fallen eighty per cent; if we do not take steps at once we will have none of our glorious air craft in the spring.

If measures are to be taken for the reestablishment of the front, I think there must not be any difference between the front and the rear! The same strong measures must be taken to save the country. In one respect there is a difference between the front and the rear; the front stands before a greater danger, and if food must be lacking any place let it be at the rear and not at the front.

I am sure that all these measures will be taken immediately, but it is not possible to take them under the pressure of defeat. If energetical measures are taken at the front to uplift the conditions there, and are considered as the result of the Tarnopol disaster and the loss of Galicia and of Bukovina, it is not admitted that order will be restored in the rear as a result of the loss of Riga, and that order will be restored on the railroads at the price of giving up Moldavia and Bessarabia to the enemy.

General Kornilov closed his speech by expressing his entire belief in the happy future for his country and in the reestablishment of the Armies, but that there is no time to waste, and that the Government must act with firmness! What a truly noble patriot! General Kornilov knew that he took his life in his hands when he made that speech; he knows that what he pleads for is a forlorn hope, and that his fate may be that of other Generals who have been murdered for expressing themselves much less plainly, yet he did his duty and told the truth. It was not necessary for him to have made a speech at all. He also knew that he had many enemies in that audience, as well as that his speech would make more.

What a shame a man like that must be sacrificed by a group of men who wish only their own comfort at the expense of no matter what! I wish I could know General Kornilov and tell him what I really think of him! It would be a great pleasure to me if of no value to him! It required exceptional bravery for him to tell the truth in that manner, when others are hiding it as loudly as they can shout! By the way, you might compare the impression you have received from my former letters with that given by the General's speech; I assure you I have not talked with him, yet he certainly expresses what have tried to tell you.

Please note that we have moved! That address at the head of this letter really means "French Quay, 8," and if you don't mind I will use that in the future! We are on the Neva, next door to the French Embassy, and I am so glad to be in this beautiful and dignified apartment, where I can receive and entertain properly.

We have attended more meetings of the St. George Cross Society, and my interest is thoroughly aroused. I do not dare write what I suspect but have an idea when some arrests are made can be less mysterious! "Princess" Kropotkin (Mrs. Lebedev)[1] seems to be taking a lively interest in the meetings. Her father is the Prince Kropotkin who was in exile many years and lived in England. While we were at one meeting Walter saw a Russian officer in a window, some distance away, using a field glass in our direction and writing something at the same time! Walter immediately went on the balcony, in plain sight of that field glass, ostensibly to smoke. I have been to the Opera and to the Musical Drama; both are excellent, but Russians tell me they have greatly deteriorated, like everything else.

Politics keep up and discipline keeps down; no less than two "counter revolutions" are in the air, but no one will tell us when they will come down to earth! Now that we are in our own quarters with some food accumulated I don't care whether they revolute or not; if they *must* shoot, I hope they will spare my gray hairs! As for politics, the Moscow Convention was a rank failure and accomplished nothing, as per my expectations.

The Germans took Riga; they took it as a grown person would take candy from a child. They can similarly take everything between Riga and Petrograd if they wish,

---

[1] The daughter of Prince Peter Kropotkin (1842–1941), the famous Russian anarchist.

but I am still of the opinion they will not make the effort now. I can find no one here who can assign a reason for the entire loss of manhood on the part of most Russian soldiers. The retired Generals with whom I talk speak of the soldiers as a loving mother might speak of a child, carefully raised, but suddenly "gone to the bad" without known reason.

General Kornilov's speech makes this letter quite long, but he expressed so many of my sentiments I could not resist putting it in. The word "situation" is beginning to bore me; I hear it so often here, but nothing else quite expresses it, so I will say: "The situation remains the same, only more so!" We have a joke: There is one here, prominent in Diplomatic Circles, who prides himself on seeing the "bright side" always. When he announces that everything is going fine; a revolution breaks or Tarnopol falls or Riga is captured! Now, when he says nothing will happen today we look for our cyclone cellars!

With our usual affectionate greetings.

Yours.

Chapter VII
ANOTHER REVOLUTION

French Quay, 8,
Petrograd,
September 14, 1917.

My dear—

Well—there has been plenty of excitement during the past week but little has happened except to a relatively small number of people! Petrograd is a busy little place, I assure you. A great many people have left the city with all their personal effects, and all exits are crowded. Railroad transportation is more in demand than ever. I cannot understand why they leave Petrograd as they do for we hear of nothing but disorders all over Russia, and I can learn of no locality that is really *safe*. In the meantime Walter has made plans for a means of escape for the American Colony, in case an escape becomes necessary. Times are uncertain and threats are many; we *may* have to run some day; it is certainly better to have a plan than to have no plan.

The Red Cross Mission had a farewell dinner at the Hotel Europe and many members leave for home very soon, the remaining few staying here to carry on their work. The American Red Cross Mission to Rumania has been represented here by a few of its members, also, so you see we have had quite a number of fine Americans about.

We have experienced considerable military and political activity (amongst Russians), the "revolution" part being about as follows: (a) General Kornilov demanded full military power; (b) Kerensky refused; (c) Kornilov said he would take it; (d) Kerensky later arrested Lvov, whom he sent with a message to Kornilov, also many members of the Duma, and others; (e) Kornilov Forces, mostly Cossacks, start for Petrograd; (f) Clashes between Kerensky and Kornilov forces; (g) Martial law proclaimed in Petrograd; (h) Everything looks like Kornilov wins easily; (i) Kornilov loses!

The political events have been too numerous to list, but the most important item would be that all but four Ministers resigned after "Kornilov's Revolution" failed, and Kerensky is stronger than ever. I am still strong for Kornilov, in spite of his failure, and I believe him to be a true patriot. I wish I could believe the same of Kerensky! There are many *dark* rumors and a rather settled conviction that General Kornilov has been "double crossed" (I hate that term, but that's what they all say!) by Kerensky. Kornilov was certainly deserted by many he had a right to suppose would uphold him in his great effort to save Russia. I have read considerable about General Kornilov, his history and career, and no one will be able to convince me he is a traitor, as he has been branded by Kerensky. Read again the speech of General Kornilov in my last letter; is that the language of a traitor? *Never*!

The net result of this last effort is that Russia is worse off than ever, and we have been shown that many who promised to assist General Kornilov in his supreme effort turned at the last moment and also turned traitors, for General Kornilov was Russia's last hope. I have seen enough now to be firmly convinced that this country will go from bad to worse until foreign aid in sufficient force cleans it up.

Kornilov is said to be a prisoner, but I will only believe that when convinced that *all* the Cossacks have turned Bolshevik! Some of those stationed in Petrograd have been contaminated, and I am not surprised at that, for some educated Americans have been that same, much to my surprise and disgust, but it *will* be a shock to me if the majority of the Cossacks give up all their traditions and become the brutes their fellows in the Army have become. General Alexiev[1] is Commander-in-Chief now, but what General Kornilov could not accomplish will not be done by the new Commander. He will only last a short time in his high office.

The women soldiers have been more than ever in evidence; they now sing as they march about the city, a custom among Russian troops. They claim to be strong for Kerensky; I trust them to remain honest in their convictions more than I trust any of the men soldiers!

There are the usual thousands of rumors, but one that seems true, and difficult to explain is that General Krimov,[2] who was believed to be in active command of the forces proceeding to Petrograd in favor of General Kornilov was ordered to Petrograd, arrived, had a consultation with Kerensky, then committed suicide. *Why?*

I must give you one example to show you why I do not enthuse over Kerensky—why I doubt his ability and motives.

When the Leninites (Anarchists) took Petrograd in July, Kerensky ordered the Cossacks out against them; when the Cossacks were reported nearing Petrograd to establish a Military Government, it was said, "Kerensky armed the Anarchists against the Cossacks." I have heard such an exhibition called "carrying water on both shoulders." Some Russians (and others) now boldly denounce Kerensky. By the way, the anarchists will not give up the arms and ammunition with which they have

---

[1] General Mikhail Alekseyev (1857–1918) was the last chief of staff and former commander in chief of the Russian Imperial Army, and then commander in chief under the Provisional Government. After the revolution, he fought against the Bolsheviks and died of heart failure.

[2] General Alexander Krymov (1871–1917) had fought in the Russian army in the Russo-Japanese War and World War I. During the Kornilov Affair of August 1917, when the Provisional Government sought protection from a feared Bolshevik coup d'etat, Krymov was in charge of troops marching on Petrograd. When the entire episode ended in confusion, Krymov was distraught at the impending Bolshevik success and committed suicide.

recently been furnished by the Kerensky Government; they will keep them, and we will hear from them when they are ready to make a noise.

The recent excitement gave the soldier-murderers another chance to slake their thirst for blood and there have been many more officers murdered. Shooting is common in the streets but no one seems to know what it is all for. Probably it is being done by *armed criminals* taking advantage of the conditions to ply their trades of murder and robbery.

Our newspapers from the States annoy me very much! They have the most misleading articles about Russia in them. How I should like to reply to some of those articles and give real facts! Of course, by the time such replies could reach an editorial desk they would be ancient history, for no one not a stenographer can really keep Russian history up to date, although, by changing names and dates, much that has happened here since my arrival would be described by histories of events here one hundred, two hundred, three hundred years ago!

Our mail service grows worse and worse, in fact we have nothing that deserves the name of "service," but I have been fortunate in being able to send out some of my letters by friends, not all of them Americans, leaving for more healthy locations; I hope you will receive all of them, for I want some of you, at least, to know what is really going on here.

I am keeping copies of all the letters, for I will find them interesting proof hereafter, to convince myself that certain things really did happen! We even find ourselves today wondering if what we saw yesterday really did take place!

Recently a French aviation officer who had fought with the Russians for two years was murdered by Russian soldiers in a most brutal manner and no real reason for it. It looks as though none of the Allies will be safe here very long. However, we may be safe for weeks, months, even years; queer people, these Russians, they acknowledge it!

For several hours during the "last revolution" no "Russian Government" could be located; so many believed that Kornilov would succeed almost without effort that Ministers were not very prominent—in fact none could be found for a time! The Allied Ambassadors and Ministers have been meeting often lately; we live quite near three Embassies and I can see the diplomats when they arrive. I have heard the Diplomatic Corps offered to mediate between the opposing factions. Walter says this again reminds him of other revolutions he has seen!

The press in Petrograd is a joke; only what is permitted by the government is published; much of it we *know* to be false, so we suspect the remainder.

We have just received some very fine mail written in July; you see the question of real correspondence is quite impossible.

In spite of the revolution my first "day" in my new home was very well attended and many were made happy by the chocolate cake I am able to supply with my tea. It is really a pleasure to see some of the Russians at tea; they so enjoy sugar, butter, jam, white bread, and the many other things they cannot get at all, and we would not have if we had not brought them with us.

I have been to the opera and the ballet again; they are still wonderful, but one takes chances in going out at night; to see the Russian opera and ballet is worth a chance or two! I shall never tire of them, but, alas—their days are numbered—I am afraid they must go, with all else that is attractive here; all is going fast.

Very many thanks for the lovely letter I had from you in the last mail, and for the newspaper clippings. I will write more briefly and intimately to you in a letter not one of this series.

In the meantime,
Affectionately yours.

French Quay, 8,
Petrograd,
September 22, 1917.

My dear—

Another very busy week, but with no revolutions. We have had a great variety of weather, including some that was very bad, and now I am sure the Germans will not get here until it freezes. They have some country to pass over between here and Riga that the rains will ruin for their purposes, and the "old inhabitants" tell me the rains are here to stay until cold weather.

There is much talk about the Capital being moved to Moscow and many believe it will be moved; I do not believe it! There is also considerable conversation about the advisability of the ladies connected with our Embassy going there now, for greater safety; some say Moscow will be safer than Petrograd, but I do not believe that—rather the contrary—and I am not going. To me it seems most probable this seat of government will retain respect for foreigners longer than any other city. Habit is strong. I fully believe the Capital will stay here. However, it all shows you that some people here think I am in danger, but please don't anybody lose any sleep over that because I am so strangely calm and certain of my safety that I simply *can't* be wrong about it!

Rear-Admiral Stanley,[3] of the British Navy, is here with his staff, and they form a very welcome addition to our colony. They are only here temporarily, but we are grateful for that. The presence of real men is a great comfort, for it seems there are so few in Russia *now*!

The customary political rumors have increased in number and importance, while Kerensky's popularity seems to have decreased. There is something about him

---

[3] Victor Stanley (1867–1934) was an officer in the British Royal Navy who commanded a squadron of battleships at the Battle of Jutland and then served as naval attaché in Petrograd.

and his dealings that makes me dubious. In this connection I am so glad to find that my American friend of the Siberian Railway journey, Mrs. Corse, who has lived so long in Russia, quite agrees with me about the relative safety of Petrograd and Moscow, as well as about all other matters affecting the "situation" here!

Since I last wrote you I have given a luncheon and two large dinner parties. You see I am taking advantage of my charming quarters and our reserve of provisions. It is my theory that when all is so solemn and threatening I must do my part towards furnishing opportunities to my friends for temporarily forgetting their troubles and those of Russia. I shall entertain as much as possible and shall have this home one where all my friends may find warmth, comfort and cheer at least once each week.

We have news that the provisions we ordered from New York are on their way to Archangel, but we had a shock when we learned that our generous (to other nations) government is charging us for freight! The total bill for provisions is about $10,000. The freight we must pay on that amount is $4,049!!! And this, mind you, when it is all consigned to officials or employees of our government! Of course that is only the ocean freight, as far as Archangel. The freight charges from there to Petrograd, the transportation in Petrograd, theft en route, and other losses, will be considerable, so we will feel quite wealthy when we are consuming the consignment, but the most important part will be the consumption!

Our work at the Lazaret continues and we are doing propaganda by sending men who have been wounded to their homes with many comforts for them and for their families. It is only a question of time when we must close the American Lazaret, but while it is open every friend we can make for the United States is well worth the effort. There must be *some* with a sense of gratitude, though the wild tales heard of crimes against owners of estates leads one to doubt it very often.

Walter attended a most elaborate stag dinner at one of the restaurants given by a Russian who is called the "Wheat King." He is reported to be enormously rich though his father was a *serf* and a glance at the menu of that dinner indicates that he must be rich! I did not even know that such a variety of food existed; one can certainly not find it in the markets so again it is proven that with wealth in Russia much can be accomplished.

There have recently been more murders of officers by their men and a particularly sad case is reported from Helsingfors, where four fine young officers were simply stood in line and shot, with no previous trial nor assigned reason! You can imagine the feelings of mothers with officer sons, and of wives whose husbands are in these mockeries of an Army and a Navy. A circular has been issued by the "Dogs' Deputies," in which they "beg, implore and order" the soldiers to cease murdering their officers. There is no mention of punishment for past murders, nor for those to come. The murders will not cease.

Everything has been so quiet in Petrograd that something big must be about to happen. It is the rule here that a calm always precedes a storm.

We have received considerable belated mail during the past week, with good news, though old news, of all our nearest relatives. It is astonishing how such a mail clears the mental atmosphere! I would not have believed reading a few letters could make such a difference. Some of the letters were twelve weeks old, but even those are new to us. The snap-shots of Paul and his horse "Jeff" appeal to us very much and it is fine to have them.

There is much talk now about Russia making a separate peace with Germany, but from our point of view I cannot see that it matters whether or not Russia signs a peace treaty. If I were asked to tell *who*, or what government in Russia can now make peace or perform any other function of a sovereign state, I could not answer the question to my own satisfaction. The *power* is one place and the alleged government another. Russia is not now in the war, except insomuch as she is assisting the Hun, so it matters little about "a scrap of paper"!! (That's what it will be if Russian representatives sign it, and we already know how Germany considers a treaty!)

More and more our friends here, Russian and foreign, who have believed they understood Russian character, tell us they are at a total loss to understand what is now going on. Peasants that were always peaceful and happy go wild and commit horrible crimes; soldiers, *always brave* and *respectful*, run amuck and in a cowardly manner torture and murder their officers; workmen without education become impressed with their abilities as statesmen and do things that would be ludicrous if not so serious; educated men of proven bravery commit suicide to escape it all! What a mess!

Recently in Finland a group of soldiers forcibly removed twenty-two officers from a train and, after torturing them unspeakably, murdered them. Not one of the soldiers was hurt! Who *can* understand such a mental attitude? By the way, after the murder of the four young men on the ship at Helsingfors, Petrograd sent an order to that ship to arrest the murderers and send them to Petrograd. The "Sailors' Committee" of the ship replied that all the twelve hundred men now living on the ship were equally responsible, so no one would be arrested! And what exists here is called a Provisional *Government*!

If my sojourn in Russia teaches me nothing more, it has taught me the danger of mob rule, and from now on I am an enemy to anything that savors of uneducated persons having the power to dictate to those who are educated. By education I do not refer alone to what one learns from school books; I mean educated in the broader sense of the word. The great crime of this situation is that, in *print* the principles alleged as the end to be attained are reasonable, sometimes good, and you would subscribe to many of them; there is enough of truth in them to make them dangerous. A certain percentage of educated people, misled by the principles in print, uphold the movement because of those principles, but I beg you to believe me when I say that it will not, *cannot*, work out as per principles unless the mob is *forced* to adhere to them, and the animal instinct curbed by the same force. The opportunity to observe *results* here has been unique and quite complete; there can be no doubt in the normal minds of reasonable observers of the complete failure of *this kind* of Democracy!

It pleases me so much to look in our courtyard and see our wood-pile. We will now be able to keep partly warm all the time and comfortably warm sometimes. We are interested to know whether the Russians who live under us will return to occupy their apartment this winter; you can readily realize that, in Russia, it makes considerable difference in one's comfort whether or not there is a cold-storage plant under the floor of one's apartment!

I am hoping and trying to keep repetitions out of my letters, but it is not easy to do, on account of that historical similarity I mentioned, which applies to weeks as well as to centuries. After all there is nothing here to write about but the "situation" (that word *must* repeat), details of which certainly are repeated, even while being augmented.

I must leave you now; I am really very busy, though accomplish but little.

Yours,

No. 8 French Quay,
Petrograd,
September 29, 1917.

My dear Susan:

The air this past week has been so tense one could feel it! Only this evening a Russian friend who is, am sure, deep in the intrigues, called us by telephone and insisted that Walter get a guard of Cossacks for this apartment! He expressed his great appreciation but will not ask for a guard. It shows what Russians themselves believe.

I have given two more dinner parties (there were five nations represented at one of them), have been out twice to dinner, and have been to the opera and to the ballet; also, my Thursday at home was the largest yet; must again increase the allowance of chocolate cake! So, you see we are busy in more ways than one.

Your letter of July first came September 13th; yours written July 25th was received today. For some unknown reason many mail pouches have been side-tracked. You know as well as we the why-fore—both of us in ignorance—but the belated mail was a great joy. So much exists about which I would like to write but *cannot*! We rehash daily so much of what has been, what is or might be, that we grow to be a sort of nightmare to ourselves. Strenuous, yes; brave, yes—so is the child who does not fear darkness because he knows not the meaning of fear. The situation here is so dark, so mysterious, and all is so upset, that anything is possible. The last storm-burst bids fair to be of long duration.

However, I am beginning to feel like the fatalist; I can see no prevention which can be applied in a moment, and as usual I am so thoroughly occupied that I have no time to court the gloom with which I assure you the air is impregnated.

There are days when the shortage of food threatens to be a wee bit more short and our wits become shortened as a consequence, for the moment only, to react with greater violence—the gods provide—and the heavens open and rain flour, butter, eggs, meal, and such, for a little while. Then comes some mail from you with ginger snaps, cocoa and soap in it! All of us lucky enough to get these precious packages gather them up as if they were the last and hide them tenderly away with watchword of "care" to our domestics.

The Russian servants have never had to guard anything, so they really cannot appreciate the appealing words, and what scarcity means. This was once a land of plenty and about as cheap as Japan used to be. Just at present, when we have made a great outlay for provisions from America, and have laid in $500.00 worth of wood, a critical turn has taken place in the affairs of Russia and this bids fair to be the most serious moment of all. It may be that someone will yet adjust the affairs of Russia but I assure you there is hardly an intelligent person here who does not feel that events are casting shadows; dark and gloomy they look.

The Bolsheviks, also called Maximalists, are feeling stronger. The July revolution was brought about by this organization, when they showed great determination to carry their willpower by arming themselves. It took, as I told you, the Cossacks to put that trouble down.

If present rumors are correct the question of what tomorrow, or the week, or the month, may bring forth is serious. Perhaps the Bourgeoisie were planning some kind of a revolution, perhaps they still are. We all feel sure that the intelligent ones of Russia are not going to allow the illiterates and working men to dictate the laws, yet Petrograd, where so much of this dictating is going on, does not represent Russia, but it is the city which seems to be paving the way to what they may call Russia's triumph, but, in reality, is her destruction.

It is more commonly believed and the belief expressed now, that the Bolsheviks, or Maximalists, or anarchists, are paid by Germany; from where else can they get the large sums of money they possess? It is positively known to Walter that there are Germans here, and they are working with those who plot the complete downfall of Russia. Are they merely renegades, or are they ordered here by those who tried to ruin all of Europe!

The Cossacks seem to be still the only dependable troops, but the terms lately applied to several of their leaders, such as "traitor" and the like, have fired that proud spirit within them, so that most of them, apparently, will go towards the South and leave Petrograd to fight her next battle alone.

Kornilov, that brave General, knows that German influence is at work somewhere, undermining the foundation of his country, and he made an effort to rally the patriotic citizens around him. The messenger, Lvov, whom I mentioned before, and who was the representative of the Church Synod,[4] holding a position in the Cabinet, evidently is a conspicuous link in the mysterious chain of failure! Probably I shall never really *know*!

The representatives of the Allied Powers have been holding daily meetings to consider how they can work a way out of this muddle. The revelation of this stupendous plot has only given the German agitators a chance to fire up again, while the fall of Riga has given the patriotic Russians the opportunity to accuse soldiers on the front of being bought over, and some go so far as to say that Kerensky and some of his Cabinet are sympathizers with Germany. *As he is a Russian Socialist*, and they are for peace at any price, you can imagine how eagerly some citizens are jumping at the truth of this.

The intriguing of the Russians is so advanced you can call it high art.

Many more people continue to leave Petrograd; some go to Moscow and some further south, but we think that very few large cities, if any, will afford protection; in fact, even the small places that have been safe are becoming dangerous on account of the flood of soldiers who have deserted from the front and are seeking a *free* life; a life where everything is free and where there is no work.

All kinds of efforts are being made to reconcile the many parties but we can only sit and wait developments. One feels so helpless when seeing such approaching destruction, without a single facility to avert calamity. Possibly a hidden rabbit feels that way when he hears heavy footsteps approaching!

The British have requested through the papers all of their subjects to notify their Consulate, within three days, of their address, telephone number, occupation, etc., giving full particulars regarding the members of their families present. In today's paper the following appears: "The Department of State desires to obtain a census of American citizens residing abroad July 1, 1917. All American citizens residing in Petrograd should call at the Consulate and communicate their addresses, with names of their families, occupation, telephone numbers, etc." All those whose duties permit them to go are being sent away. All Embassies are planning for the escape of those who must remain. There is no fear of the Germans coming soon, but a serious Bolshevik uprising is anticipated, and its success means *Anarchy*.

Walter has chartered a steamer large enough to accommodate the entire American Colony, and she is lying in the Neva, with steam up, ready to start for Lake Ladoga and "points north"! He conceived this idea when he saw the great strain that was being put on all means of transportation, and recognized that, should the necessity for flight arise, there would be no transportation. He brought the matter to the attention of those who must decide, got maps of the country to the north, and sent two reliable men over the route he picked out as practicable. They returned and reported that the scheme is all right and that they had made arrangements for a special train

---

[4] The Church Synod was a government organization that oversaw church affairs.

at the end of water navigation. You would be surprised to learn of the great effort required to get the plan finally settled and the steamer in readiness, but now that all members of the Colony know there is an immediate chance of escape they are greatly relieved. The steamer is provisioned and armed and is guarded by volunteers who stand watches on board.

The latest rumor that affects us personally is to the effect that the Bolsheviks are planning for the destruction of the Allies here represented, but probably that is only another form of terrorization, which is their stock in trade. The Americans are prominently mentioned for special attention, but we look upon that as an effort on the part of the Hun to reduce the favor in which we have generally been held by the Russians.

The Russians with handsome homes live in daily terror of being driven out of them, as some have already been driven. You will remember the story I told you of the palace occupied by the secretaries from our Embassy, the one they reached in time to prevent the soldiers from taking it; there is another story of that palace, which runs like this:

The Americans are wealthy and each has his valet; the valet of one of them organized a band to rob the palace, the plan including the chloroforming and possibly injuring the three men. One of the confederates became conscience stricken and gave the plan away to the owner of the palace, who took steps to save his valuables, of which there were many and some rare ones. Only two of the Americans were at the palace; the other, whose valet was the ringleader, being on leave in Scandinavia, and the two were informed of the plot. One night one of them was awakened after a restless sleep caused by the uneasiness of his dog, by feeling a cold hand on his face, but he could not detect the odor of chloroform and was less excited when the voice of his fellow occupant said, "They are here, I am going for my gun!" They waited, fully prepared to fight, and soon saw a light under a bathroom door, which varied in intensity; soon that door was opened slowly and the two were ready to show what Americans can do when the electric torch was turned on them and the owner of the palace said: "It is all right, we caught thirteen of them!" The valet who had organized the raid had told his fellow friends that his master was in Scandinavia ready to receive and dispose of the goods where it was to be taken in a chartered yacht. We had fun with the one who had been on leave when he returned!

The latest allowance gives each person one half pound of bread per day, but as we cannot eat that bread, and have some expensive flour, it does not interest us, from a selfish point of view. How does flour at $36.00 per barrel appeal to you? We would pay any price to get it! A consistent rumor that does annoy us is that the electric light is to be out off; there is reason to believe it, for the fuel supply is very low and the transportation cannot deliver more. It is certain that the electric lights will not continue through the winter, and, as one needs them nearly all day, we are planning for candles and kerosene light. With our food from New York is some kerosene which will be a lifesaver for lamps and stoves!

You and Richard are so kind—we appreciate everything you do for us and often talk about you; we miss you both very much. By the way, disabuse your mind of the impression you have that Walter is sorry I am here! He says he would be hopelessly miserable and does not know what he would do if I were not here; my being here is the one thing that makes it bearable. He says further that my help to him in getting information could not be duplicated by anyone he knows, for, on Thursday evenings, when we compare notes, he can state right accurately what is in the air! He also states that his conceit permits him to believe he can take good care of me; naturally he would not have me stay if he thought there was immediate danger, and he feels that he will take better care of me than any other person would! So, I stay, and I am glad of it.

A great many of our friends in the States do not yet know where we are, for we left in a hurry, with more or less secrecy, and "orders to officers" were not being printed when we left. I will be glad if you will let as many as convenient know where we are. I just received an invitation to a luncheon in New York which took place two months ago and am wondering what the hostess thinks of me; other similar aged invitations have been received here.

How I wander on!! I had no idea this letter was so long! I have not been disturbed while writing it, which is unusual, but I will not write more now.

With much love from both,

French Quay, 8,
Petrograd,
October 4, 1917.

My dear—

It seems there may be an opportunity to send mail tomorrow, so I will sit up late tonight and have this ready to send to you. So much has happened (yet really nothing vital), I am again at a loss to know what to leave out!

The day after I last wrote you the Anarchists had an open meeting near their headquarters, across the river, to denounce the United States and to protest against the activities there against their brother Anarchists and the I.W.W.'s. Walter had a "scout" at the meeting who reported that the "Chairman" began the party by welcoming "Brothers, Comrades and *Spies* from the American Embassy"! That same day our Embassy had a guard consisting of an armored car and fifty soldiers sent by the Provisional Government (without a request having been made for it), so you see it is evident that all the threats made against Americans have convinced those in power here there may be some danger for us. What a reversal of form, and how clever of our enemies to have brought it about! Also, how helpless we are to combat it! Naturally, it makes no difference to the few Americans here—that is not the idea—it is our country that will suffer in the long run, and with the same ammunition the Germans are using it would be possible to retain the friendship that really did exist for the United States!

There is sadness in the family of my dear little interpreter friend; her brother, a fine handsome lad of nineteen, has completed his course at the Military School and has gone to the Riga Front as an officer of artillery; any front is very unsafe for officers now, not because of the German enemy, but because of the more dangerous Russian soldiers. What a shame to sacrifice these fine young men to the blood thirst of the human beasts! I could weep!

Bad weather is here in earnest now—cold, raw, windy and wet, and that will make it difficult for the Germans to advance far towards Petrograd, a fact that some Russians, though they hate the Germans, regret because they know the Germans would establish order and curb the activities of those whose single aim seems to be to make everybody unhappy but themselves. They have said in speeches anyone could hear that they would reduce the better classes to a crust of bread and bare feet. Is that *Socialism*?

The Germans have taken Oesel Island and other small islands about Riga Gulf —to tighten their hold on Riga, no doubt. That is where I was invited to visit, and while I would have been away before the capture, I would not have enjoyed the daily bombing by aeroplanes the Huns gave the place for a long time before they captured it. Walter was in one raid there and I am afraid he enjoyed it.

Politically the most important event has been the success of the Bolsheviks (anarchists) in keeping the "Kadets" out of the Ministry. This is significant because it shows the increasing power of the awful Bolsheviks!

We have dined out three times, once at the French Embassy, and I had one dinner party at home. It was fortunate I increased my chocolate cake ration for many callers were here today in spite of bad weather and bad politics.

We had an experience on the street during one of our walks that will show you considerable concerning the peculiar mental attitude of the Russian peasant. We saw some desirable looking apples; price, one ruble fifty kopecks (about fifteen cents in our money just now) each; I decided to take five of them; the woman selling them *would not accept five times the value of one*! While this roused our ire and we decided not to buy, we discussed the experience, and approached three other women selling apples, with the same result in each case. They argue if you want two apples you want them about twice as badly as you want one; if you want *five* you want them considerably more than five times as badly as you want one, therefore you must pay eight (about) times as much! Not one of those four apple women would sell us five apples for five times the price at which they would sell one, so we assumed it could not have been ignorance on the part of anyone, nor a coincidence! Please tell me how to argue with people like that!

Feeling against the Allies continues to grow; that is not a coincidence, either; the German agents are active and efficient. Two incidents that happened to Americans will illustrate: An American lady, Mrs. Hutchins, was approached by a drunken Russian soldier who, after some effort, succeeded in putting his arm around her; quite a crowd saw the whole affair, and while she managed to get away from the soldier, not one of the men who saw it raised a hand! That lack of protection for a lady I would not have believed possible in any capital in the world. A young American was riding on a street car; he wore a good-looking sweater which a Russian workman insisted upon buying. When finally convinced that the American would not sell it, the workman said: "Never mind—you are an American—soon I will cut your throat and take the sweater!" Such an incident could not have happened a short time ago.

We are now reading *alleged* interviews with Americans in some of our newspapers, and Oh! how they discourage us! To think that the American people should be so deceived! As a mere item: We read that "Russian soldiers are returning to the trenches," and probably many Americans believe that. As a matter of fact about two million Russian soldiers have deserted during the past month. I could write pages giving similar proof that what you have been reading is not true, but I have not the time to do it and the assurance of good to be accomplished that way is lacking also.

Madame Egorev, the wife of an officer in the Russian Admiralty, and I have become good friends; she is a dear sweet woman; she has just told me of *their* troubles, somewhat as follows: Her husband was ordered by the "Secretary of the Navy" to move into a certain apartment in the Admiralty building, he having previously occupied a private apartment some distance therefrom. The "Sailors' Committee" which is running the Navy Department announced that it wanted that apartment, the one into which Captain Egorev was ordered to move, for its use, and that Captain Egorev could not have it. Kerensky and the Secretary of the Navy "dissolved" the "Sailors' Committee" and ordered it out of the Admiralty building. The committee replied that it refused to be dissolved, it would occupy the apartment in question, would kill Captain Egorev if he moved into it, and, furthermore, demanded his immediate "dismissal" from the Admiralty, and from his important position therein, as well as that of his Chief, Captain Romanov.

We are informed by the newspapers that the "Government" has *compromised* with the Committee, and this is how they did it:

1. The Committee is not dissolved.
2. It occupies the apartment wanted.
3. Captains Romanov and Egorev have been dismissed.

I also read some wonderful eulogies of Kerensky in our press, and I wonder who inspires them. They are certainly not warranted by *any results* he has brought about. He has apparently arranged his own personal affairs rather satisfactorily for him, but what has he done for Russia? What for the Allies?

The wonderful "free speech" here one reads about is only free for the man with a gun. Newspaper articles which do not please the man with the gun are suppressed—censored; those which please him but not the editor are printed at the point of a gun; that's how free the press is!

I regret that I could not have made collection of the hundreds of resolutions "unanimously passed" by various committees and meetings of those who are ruling Russia. They would require a trunk to hold them and I am not sure I will be able to get out with the trunks I have. They would certainly convince anyone with a normal brain that the "Russian idea" is all wrong, but I need only to ask you to look at the results and to observe how this magnificent country has been ruined and is being driven to further ruination each day.

The French Embassy has also chartered a steamer for use if they must escape. It is secured to the river quay just under our front windows, while the American steamer is above the last bridge so there will be no drawbridge complications if her use becomes necessary. I believe the British Embassy has a similar plan, but their problem is a much larger one because the number of their citizens here is so great. Naturally, none of us want to go off on an "escape party," but it is a great comfort to be ready to try, if a necessity arises. The possibilities here are great; nothing can happen and *everything* can also.

Don't forget how we long for mail!

With love,

P. S.—The following official telegram shows what demoralization existed in October, 1917:

Front broken!

General Bonch-Bruevich,[5] the Commander-in-Chief's Chief of Staff, has sent the following urgent telegram to Krylenko[6] (a former second lieutenant and now Commander-in Chief):

"Complete *anarchy* prevails. Many portions of the front are denuded. On the Western Front only 160 rifles per verst can be reckoned upon. The reserves are not relieving their comrades in the trenches. A large number of experienced military leaders have left on behalf of the elections. The present officers' corps is inexperienced. The staffs and institutions will soon cease work automatically, for there is no one to do the work. There is no

---

[5] General Vladimir D. Bonch-Bruyevich (1873–1955) was a member of the Petrograd Military-Revolutionary Committee and became executive secretary in Lenin's first government in the fall of 1917, drafting the decree on the nationalization of the banks in Russia.

[6] Nikolai V. Krylenko (1885–1938) was a Bolshevik lawyer given the position of commissar of war in Lenin's first government in the fall of 1917. He later became commissar of justice and was instrumental in setting up the Soviet legal system and drafting the first constitutions of the new Soviet government. He was executed in 1938 during Stalin's purges.

one at Headquarters. The working conditions at the Staffs are terrible. The Commissariat has broken down completely. Drill and order among the troops are null. There is no military discipline. Orders are not executed. Desertion is taking place en masse. Men on leave are not returning. Touch is lost in many localities. The cavalry is almost annihilated. Fortified positions are being destroyed. Barbed wire entanglements have been removed to facilitate fraternization and trading with the enemy. It is impossible to withstand any attack from the enemy. The only salvation for the army is to retreat to the natural boundaries."

No. 8 French Quay,
Petrograd,
October 14, 1917.

My dear—

This time there is really nothing of interest, and I am so afraid of tiring you by repeating, as I am often made weary here by "the situation," "food," "politics" and "murders"! The Germans have continued their successes about Riga Gulf and we are beginning to learn details of the farce of a defense put up by the Russians there. Certainly their "freedom" has not made brave men of them!

There have been the usual numbers of dinners, etc., and I had my largest "Thursday" yet—there being seven nations represented by my guests. I have also been to the ballet again. We received a particularly interesting mail from home, with much good news, including that of Walter's promotion!

We have experienced a dense fog in Petrograd, accompanied by so much smoke from burning forests that it *hurt the eyes*. It almost makes me ill to think of the burning forests when so many cannot get enough wood for cooking!

Anarchy in general throughout Russia is on the increase, more and more cities and towns becoming involved. Petrograd is less safe. A few days ago some soldiers were abusing a crippled soldier who was selling cigarettes on the street; an Englishman who spoke Russian expostulated with them; they killed the Englishman! Robberies have increased to really an alarming extent. A band in the uniforms of soldiers simply goes to an apartment or store and loots it; no one is punished—no one is even arrested. The cook in an apartment building *next to ours* was murdered and the apartment robbed while the family was out. That is getting quite too close to home! We have heard of a mutiny in the German Fleet! It seems too good to be true, yet it is such cheerful news I believe it. Strikes here increase in number and seriousness. The latest is a *general railroad strike*, which was not needed at all to demoralize the transportation.

The journals have published elaborate directions as to what we must do when the German air raids begin. One of my witty Russian friends, Baroness Maydell,[7] says she presumes the best thing to do would be to sit still and scream!

There is a lot of work going on in connection with the official evacuation of Petrograd and the river Quay is lined with large barges being filled with archives and works of art. The famous Hermitage has been stripped, many of its wonders and articles of immense value having been stolen. One large barge-load started for Moscow; those in charge of it reported it had sunk; most likely they disposed of its contents to their own advantage! What a great shame that such a wonderful collection as the Hermitage had afforded is forever lost to the world!

There is quite a sight to be seen near the center of Petrograd, called the "Soldiers' Market"; hundreds of soldiers are there, selling almost every conceivable article, including their uniforms, boots, weapons, jewelry, paintings, statuary and other things obviously stolen by them. While interesting to look at it is also most disgusting.

The British Embassy pouch was rifled at the Finland Railroad Station and some beautiful enamel stolen. Absolutely nothing is safe or sacred now, but I cannot hold my breath in expectation that I will be the next to suffer. I try to continue in regular routine, but one's mind and conversation certainly get in a groove here!

There is a controversy on now between the "Government" and the Bolsheviks. The Government states it will move to Moscow; Bolsheviks say they will not permit the move! I am still of the opinion the move will not be made.

I am poor at figures and detest them; I believe statistics would bore you; therefore I will not delve deeply into the economic situation here. There are a few facts that will convince you of the utter failure of what some Socialists believe to be their great opportunity here. (They are really quite blind, for no one worthwhile who really *knows* what is being done in Russia will ever consider Socialism as anything but a menace!) Wages and costs of raw material in factories have increased tremendously in Russia; percentages of increases range from ten to a thousand and more, so a table would be useless to elaborate for our purposes. *But*, at the same time, the output of those same factories has *decreased enormously*, owing to *lessened efficiency* and fewer hands. (Many "workmen" find it more agreeable and more profitable to play at being soldiers in the "Red Guard," where they have little or nothing to do, the best that can be obtained to eat, and very large "wages.")

Possibly a few simple figures will illustrate. Suppose a factory before the revolution produced a thousand of its standard articles per day and made a profit of one ruble each on them; the following month each of a thousand workmen had his wages increased by a ruble per day, but did not work as many hours nor as well as he did before and the production fell to five hundred articles per day; the factory now runs

---

[7] Baroness Eveline Adelheid von Maydell (1890–1962) was a silhouette portraitist who studied in several places, including Russia.

at a *loss* of five hundred rubles per day, but the workmen will not believe it! Add to this loss the increase in the cost of raw materials and one can readily see without more figures how easy it has been to wreck the factories, and they have been *wrecked*! They can never run unless intelligence is at the head of them, and that will never be under existing conditions.

I am now convinced that General Kornilov was deliberately sacrificed by Kerensky. Understand, I believe it, but cannot prove it, for proof of such would require an accurate inside knowledge of what actually went on, whereas I can only piece together the puzzle formed by the many rumors that have persistently circulated, and from which one must eliminate many as improbable. There is reason to believe, and many do believe, that Kornilov approached Petrograd with Kerensky's knowledge and approval; that it was fully understood Kornilov was to establish a Military Government and bring order at the front and in the rear, in accordance with the statements in his speech at Moscow; that, in the evening all was arranged, and a more or less triumphant entry into Petrograd planned for Kornilov. During the night it is presumed someone or some thought suggested to Kerensky that he would lose power and prestige as Kornilov's increased. His ambition could not stand that pressure. Kerensky is well known to be hysterical; one has only to see him make a speech to be assured of that; in the early morning Kornilov was hysterically proclaimed to be a traitor and ordered arrested.

Regardless of how much truth there is in my belief, the *fact* remains that Kerensky foiled an honest attempt to save Russia, and that Russia is now worse off than ever before. No unprejudiced person can know Kornilov's history and believe him to be a traitor. I have assurance that, while Kornilov is nominally under arrest, he is surrounded by faithful Cossacks and is in no danger at all.

This assurance comes from a quarter too well informed to leave any doubt in my mind, and I am further informed by the same source that the General has not yet given up hope, and is waiting to see what his next move should be. He apparently can go where he will, but knows he would accomplish nothing by coming to Petrograd now. If any Russian can save Russia he can, but he wishes to avoid civil war and believed his attempted dictatorship had been so arranged that none would result. How very sad it all is and how one must pity these dark minds, even while despising them and while detesting the awful conditions they have brought about all over Russia.

I have a very strong intuitive feeling about it all, reinforced by considerable information, and I am forced to believe that the *cleverness* with which all this ripe mental soil has been cultivated is German-made. The destruction has been too progressive and certain to have been planned beforehand by Russian minds; the results have been too favorable to Germany to permit the belief that she has been innocent of effort. Why should we believe her innocent?

By this time every reasonable mind in the United States is aware of Germany's efforts in our own country, and it would seem without reason she should neglect the wonderful opportunity presented in Russia. Some Americans here believe anarchy may yet cross into Germany, and use the reported mutiny in their fleet as an argument; I want to believe it myself, but it would be infinitely better *to try to stop this, or any other dangerous disease, in Russia*, rather than to wish it on Germany! If it attacks the well-disciplined Germans, it can go *any*where, and a world full of Bolshevism would be a world not worth inhabiting!

If a very small portion of all we are promised in the near future actually takes place, my next letter may be more exciting. I offer my apologies for writing what looks now like an essay, but having written it, I mail it!

Best wishes, regards and love,
From

8 French Quay,
Petrograd,
October 24, 1917.

My dear—

The many things promised did not materialize and now there is a dearth of news, but it has been ten days since I last wrote to you and I feel that I must not wait longer or I will forget what happened!

I do not know when this will be mailed, for that uncertainty is ever with us now. We received another fine mail in which was the wonderful news that our Midshipman son has five stripes! Perhaps *that* does not cheer us in this cheerless Russia! We feel sad that we cannot see him with his honors, nor even be there when he is graduated, but we are hoping some of our relatives and friends will be able to attend the Graduation Exercises.

The one thing that has lessened the personal strain here, has been the excellent reports from both of our sons. That our Midshipman should have received the highest honors given at the Naval Academy shows that he has done his part. We get the most excellent reports from the Head Master at Woodberry Forest concerning the conduct and class standing of our other son, which makes us proud and happy. I am so glad our two sons could be together during their vacation. We have excellent kodak photographs of them both and of the horse, "Jeff," as well.

Walter has been quite ill with this terrible Russian grippe, and it has left him weak. It will not be one bit comfortable to be sick here, for the strongest suffer, and I hope there will be no more of it.

My Russian friends are now coming to see me frequently to inquire about the possibility of their friends being "received" in the United States! They feel so humiliated that they believe the mere fact they are Russians will prevent them from being recognized in other countries. One reason for this is the report that has come from France concerning the Russians there and the treatment they have received. I cannot do it, but I would like to answer my friends somewhat like this: "If they are good strong people they are needed in Russia; if they are not, they are not needed in the United States"! We *are* sorry for them—their case seems so hopeless; in disguise, hunted from their homes, slinking from one city to another, looking for safety! They have not really done anything, either—they are simply the victims of one bad system that has been overcome by a worse one.

We gave a very attractive dinner for the French Ambassador and Madame Noulens,[8] with sixteen present. It is permitted to comment upon what is served here, and our "American food" is a real cause for conversation. Our friends of the St. George Cross Society have given a benefit and I heard an opera singer from Moscow who is simply wonderful. I hope *she* will escape to our country! We went to see "Ivan the Terrible" played by an excellent Russian company. The play lasted five hours, but the wonderful acting, coupled with the magnificent costumes and scenery, made one forget time. I was quite surprised to learn how late it was when we left the theater.

We are now being urged by Russians to get a force of American troops here, but that effort was started by Walter some months ago and it is now a bit late, though it would be worth the trial.

Monday, October Twenty-ninth.
Some of our Red Cross Mission to Rumania are passing through here for the United States, via Siberia, and I will finish this tonight to send it by that route. I believe that insures your receiving it, and I am sorry there is not more of interest in it, but real excitement is lacking just now! It is quite interesting enough for those of us here, but if written it would read so much like what I have written before. Just now, in Petrograd papers, are appearing inspired articles in which the Russian sailors are claiming much for their "victory" over the Germans in the Riga Gulf! The Germans drove the Russians out and now occupy the Gulf; possibly the Russian sailors think they won because they were able to escape. It is a boast quite in line with another made by some soldiers who announced with pride they had murdered their General and arrested sixty of their officers.

Life remains serious here, and will continue to be so. Sometimes one forgets long enough to make a bon-mot, or to laugh at one, but it is almost a sin to think frivolously. This is the day when one must emulate shabbiness and lack of pride, if the Bolsheviks are to remain *autocrats*. How would you like a band of dark minds, in unclean clothes, leading you by the nose, or ear, as they see fit? Sometimes I wonder if I will ever again think and live in a normal way!

---

[8] Joseph Noulens (1864–1944) was French ambassador to Russia during the period 1917–18.

Now it is late; this letter is unsatisfactory to me, so it will be the same to you; possibly "the situation" is getting on my nerves, but I try to flatter myself it is not. How glad I will be to see you all!!!!

With much affection,
Your

Chapter VIII
THE BOLSHEVIK REVOLUTION

8 French Quay,
Petrograd,
November 7, 1917.

My dear—

NOW, my dear, there is some excitement, and as I write the atmosphere is punctuated by all kinds of shots—rifle, pistol, machine guns, field pieces and large guns aboard ships! Walter and Miss Gueradhy are at the telephone getting reports from various parts of the city and I am putting down my impressions while they are fresh in my mind. It is midnight, but I am not sleepy!

Yesterday Walter was at the Admiralty, making his routine visit, when his friend there advised him to get home quickly, saying: "They are going to try again, these people!" On his way home he heard much shooting and saw the bridges being opened to prevent the Anarchists from crossing them. He came to the Lazaret for me and advised the other ladies to get home as quickly as possible, further advising them to come to our house if unable to get home. After we reached our apartment we telephoned to all Americans we could reach, advising them of the trouble. There was street fighting, but not serious, and by midnight all seemed quiet, though there was an occasional shot. Mrs. Volkeapaa had been unable to reach her home so came to us for dinner. We telephoned to her husband, who managed to get to our house and later took her home.

This morning we heard that the Anarchists had repeated their effort of last July, only more successfully, and the entire city was in their possession, though fighting continued all day in the streets. Miss Gueradhy, the interpreter, very pluckily came in the morning but the fighting was too severe in the afternoon and she prepared to remain here tonight, after telephoning to her mother. There seemed to be no let-up in the fighting. We all prepared for bed, when very heavy guns were heard, and we learned by telephone that the Russian Cruiser *Aurora* is in the river, bombarding the Winter Palace. We can see the Fortress of Peter and Paul from our front windows and the flashes of field guns there, apparently also firing at the Winter Palace.

Fortunately for the information we so desire, Walter has many friends in different parts of the city to whom it has been his custom to telephone in cases like this, and tonight the system is working so he is getting reports from all of them. They indicate that fighting is general all over the city, but hardest about the Winter Palace, where it seems the most of the Ministers of the Provisional Government have taken refuge. We have been promised this uprising for several days, in fact I wrote you last July that it would come, but, believing the Government knew as much as I did, it seemed they would be prepared for it, but the city has again fallen an easy prey to the better organized anarchists, who have had some German assistance this time in their organization.

We now have a considerable store of provisions in the house and will not suffer if forced to remain indoors, though it is another item of interest here that no one stays at home simply because there is street fighting! We even go to the ballet and opera, dodging those sections of the city where we hear shooting, both going and returning. I had another large dinner party here and no one stayed away because of the fighting.

We are wondering tonight if all the various threats of the anarchists, made in their speeches during the past few months, will be carried out! The threats included making as much misery as possible for those they do not like, and I believe they have the desire and intention to do that very thing. I have not heard of any threat or plan to really better conditions, except that it has been threatened that those who live in large handsome homes must give up some of their rooms to those less fortunate. If it comes to that I hope I may have some choice as to my boarders! You should have seen us hiding our precious canned fruit, vegetables, condensed milk, cocoa, etc., we received from the States! It will take a search party a long time to locate all of it; not even our domestics know where it is.

Today one of the naval officers Walter knew at Oesel Island came here with the customary request that he be sent to the United States to serve in our Navy. There have been many rumors of what happened at Oesel Island when the Germans captured it, and this officer confirmed many of them. I will only give you one sad incident, which will convince you what horrible creatures are now in power here. The officer who invited us to visit them at Oesel Island had his wife and two beautiful children with him there, a girl and a boy. He was in command of the forces on the Island, and had made plans to remove his family if the place fell. He remained with his men during the few minutes they resisted the Germans, and followed them in their mad retreat, going to his house to take his family on board ship. What he saw in his home caused him to shoot himself; his own men, in retreating, had outraged the wife and daughter, and had murdered all three of his family. Could men be worse? Yet these are the people some Americans with brains are urging us to trust, bear with, uphold, and *acknowledge!*

Another robbery took place in our *immediate* neighborhood; a post and telegraph office was robbed, the young woman in charge at the time being brutally murdered. The number of such cases is increasing all the time, but I only give you the few as examples!

Nothing really worse than what has happened since we have been here can happen; the only way in which it will change is for a greater number of the same things to happen. Even, their fiendish ingenuity can probably not devise worse tortures than have been and are being inflicted. Of course their successes during the past two days will inflame all their passions and make times worse in the respect that more will suffer. The "searching parties," which are really "looting parties," will now have a more free hand, and their activities will increase.

It is a source of great satisfaction to me that my husband, soon after his arrival here, announced the great need for foreign troops and for propaganda; he could get no one in authority to agree with him, but he has continued his efforts and now, as if it were quite a new idea, many are saying "We must have foreign troops and active propaganda." His ability to say "I told you so" does not help the situation a bit, so he does not say it. What he does say is "You'd better hurry, or it will be too late!" Troops *could* have been brought here and successful propaganda, or rather counter-propaganda, for there was much of the German variety already, *could* have been carried on, but no one seemed to be able to see the necessity for them.

In some of our mail I read of the servant troubles in the States; I rather suspect that you are infinitely better off than we are in that respect! Probably none of your servants believe they have the *right* to murder you if they so desire!

One more of the best generals Russia had, Dukhonin,[1] has been murdered, and so they go—always the best—though Alexiev managed to be relieved by Dukhonin without being killed. The new Commander-in-Chief is a second lieutenant, who will do just as well as any, for there are no armies left to command. The latest official robbery came out a few days ago. Everyone living in an apartment the rent for which is one hundred and fifty rubles per month or more is required to furnish the robber rulers of Russia with two warm articles of clothing. As I have not seen any apartments that cheap, the order is a very general one.

At last we have a courier mail service, but that is a comfort that will not last long, for already the British Embassy has had to discontinue its couriers. Just now the Bolsheviks are particularly cross with the British because two Russians with criminal records are being held in custody in England. This simply shows that they are no respecters of persons or governments, and our turn is likely to come at any time. It is a great pleasure to see our couriers, though; fine, big, real men.

Just now we have no electric light from midnight to five in the morning, and it will soon be reduced very materially. We are ready for all reductions, except that our electric door bell is on the lighting circuit! Walter could install a bell easily enough but one cannot be found.

---

[1] General Nikolai N. Dukhonin (1876–1917) was the last commander in chief of the Russian Imperial Army, and then became chief of staff at General Headquarters at Mogilev for the Provisional Government. He refused to cooperate with Lenin's new government and was killed by a mob of Bolshevik soldiers in Mogilev in late November 1917.

Germans are thick in Petrograd now. They have offices and are "advising" the Bolsheviks, who, by the way, have taken the most famous girls' school in the country, Smolny Institute,[2] for their Headquarters. I suppose it is no secret that the Germans are here for I met one quite openly at a tea recently.

Just now I hear no shooting, and I *am* sleepy; so I will stop. There will certainly be many people leaving here now, so I will have this ready to send by the first one of whom I learn. You need not worry about us for we will be safe as long as anyone is, and there will be foreigners in Petrograd for a long time yet.

Until next time,
Yours faithfully,

8 French Quay,
Petrograd,
November 12, 1917.

My dear—

The letter I wrote you the night of the heavy firing got away the next day, but I am not making it a matter of record who took it, because no one knows who will see this letter, or whether or not it will reach you! I shall keep on writing, and take advantage of all opportunities to send something out. Such chances will decrease from now on. The heavy firing above mentioned was at "The Battle of the Winter Palace"! Said Palace was defended by a few women soldiers and some military cadets, only. Walter says he has never before seen a revolution in which the government put out of office has been defended by armed women and children alone! A few were killed and the place surrendered, all Ministers being arrested, *except Kerensky*, who fled early in an automobile commandeered from an American! He said he was going for loyal troops and would be back soon to recapture Petrograd. I will be surprised if we see him again, *for Kerensky is finished*. This is no "demonstration" such as we saw in July and I believe these people are here for a long time to come. Then there was much parading and showing of force on the streets; this time the force was here, but it was sprung suddenly in many parts of the city at the same time, with no parading at all. There has been constant fighting since I last wrote you, but no general fight in which large numbers took part; simply fights for the possession of points desired by each side, such as the great favorite, the telephone exchange, and the various public buildings.

We have been on the streets a great deal, looking for information but have escaped running into the fights. We try to avoid them! Walter has taken several long walks, accompanied by an interpreter, inspecting the "defenses" and interrogating the "defenders," so he has known accurately what has been going on. We find it dif-

---

[2] In 1764, Catherine the Great set up the first Russian school for girls: the Smolny Institute for Noble Maidens.

ficult to determine to which "side" a group of soldiers belongs without asking them. Some do not know at what nor why they shoot. They have guns and ammunition, so they shoot! We walked around the Winter Palace and saw the marks of the fray—but in spite of all the firing *we heard* and the flashes of the guns *we saw*, as well as the short distances concerned, we could only see *two* places where anything larger than a rifle bullet had hit that perfectly enormous building!

A friend said he was in front of the Palace when the Bolsheviks opened fire with a field gun at about one thousand yards range. He waited and observed that the shot missed; some Russians reeled on the cold ground and *howled* with glee; they fired several shots while he watched them and none hit! They quit firing in disgust. There are hundreds of bullet marks on the windows and walls of the Palace; it looks like a case of measles. We are told the women soldiers who were captured were distributed among several of the barracks in the city; no imagination is required to know their fate! The city is patrolled by armed bands, with the ever present armored and armed cars, as well as the joy-riding motor trucks, and one simply can't be happy under the circumstances. The absence of drunken men has heretofore been a comfort; that comfort has disappeared, and I freely confess that I am afraid of an intoxicated Russian with a gun.

My day at home was well attended *by men!* Two ladies who live in the immediate neighborhood came in early but left before it began to grow dark.

The house-to-house search "for arms" is again underway with more thoroughness than ever. Our friend Mr. Corse had to give up his pistol, but he did it under protest, demanded a receipt, and the pistol was returned to him!

News from Moscow indicates they are having the fighting simultaneously, only more bloody than Petrograd. "Peaceful Moscow"; how glad I am I did not go there! There has been severe fighting at Tsarskoe Selo, but no news of Kerensky. We hear that a "Provisional Government Army" will soon recapture Petrograd; I will believe that when I see the city in other hands, for I believe the Bolsheviks are now here to stay!

Considerable firing was going on in the city all day yesterday and we heard several shots of field pieces. One sad affair took place; the "Junkers," (Military Cadets, mere boys) captured the telephone exchange, a place where there is always a fight, from the Bolsheviks early in the morning; they were not reinforced as per plan, ran out of ammunition and gasoline for their armored cars, and in the afternoon the Bolsheviks recaptured the place, killing many of the Junkers and mutilating their bodies in their rage. These Junkers correspond to our West Point cadets, but are much younger; they generally represent the best families of Russia; so many of them have been killed![3]

---

[3] Crosley accurately describes junkers as junior military officers of noble background who were opposed to the Bolsheviks.

We have been without telephone service a great deal, but today we may telephone to Russian or foreign *offices*—not to private apartments. The head of the American Railroad Commission, Mr. Stevens,[4] is living in his private car in the railroad yards at Moscow; he writes that there is much shooting in Moscow and that he is unable to accomplish anything! (He is a fine man, but he might as well go home and work with our own railroads!)

Again there has been no government in Petrograd; no one with whom foreigners could do business; the city has been in the possession of armed soldiers, sailors and workmen, many of them intoxicated, and there was a total inability to detect who, in any given group, is the leader thereof. There *appears* to be no organization, no responsibility, though of course a great deal centers in Smolny, which is a very busy place, bristling with machine guns and others. Walter does not go there but his "scouts" do, so we know what it looks like.

As an example of the armed bands: This morning one of these was strolling up the Quay when a Russian officer came along; nothing was said, but one of the band raised his rifle, fired, and the officer fell dead. The band moved on without comment and without even a glance at the corpse! My friend who saw it and related the incident to me is not certain murder was intended, but is certain there was no good reason for the crime. Think of Petrograd being in the hands of such a heartless mob!

The recent prohibition of street corner meetings is of course a dead issue now and many are the impromptu speeches one hears. All have the same theme and are intended to inflame the bandits against those who occupy comfortable homes and have things to eat. They are advised that now *everything* is common property, to be searched out and seized when discovered, and that whatever force is found necessary may be applied! How about our stores of expensive provisions from New York? Common property? Oh, no?

In our strolls along the river we counted nine naval vessels of different types, which were used to bring soldiers, sailors and others from Helsingfors and Kronstadt. The opening of the draw-bridges by the Provisional Government forces had little effect, all the anarchists needed on this side of the river having come over in small groups before they started their fireworks; also, the naval vessels were used as ferries. Oh! They were well advised *this* time!

Two days ago "Commissaires" were sent around to the Embassies with messages that the revolution had failed, and the Provisional Government was again in complete control. While the messages were being delivered there was still much shooting, and of course there was no truth in the statements—quite the contrary—and now we are trying to figure out the why of the hoax!

---

[4] John F. Stevens (1853–1933) was appointed by the US State Department as chairman of the American Railroad Commission, which was given the task of assisting in the improvement of transportation facilities of the Siberian railway, because at that time, Russia was an ally.

In *August* I stoutly affirmed that the days of Kerensky and his power were numbered; no one agreed with me and some took me to task for making such a "pessimistic" statement; while it is not yet really confirmed, my conviction remains that he is now only an unpleasant memory which will grow less pleasant as facts concerning him become better known.

Many of the streets are still barricaded and we have to dodge the barricades as well as the fights when we go for our strolls, thereby adding to the exercise and the interest. There are the usual number of wild rumors, many insisting that large bodies of Cossacks are approaching Petrograd from several directions, and that very soon "the streets will run deep with the blood of anarchists"! I am sorry I cannot believe it! I have heard considerable of how the Cossacks feel, and the fiasco of last July, coupled with the treatment given their great Kornilov, has made them doubt the honesty of the Provisional Government, and I will be greatly surprised if the Cossacks sacrifice any of their numbers for Kerensky.

The name of Lenin is prominent, as before, but also one Trotsky (Bronstein) is now in the limelight. He has been "elected" Foreign Minister, and his strong point seems to be making bloodthirsty speeches. We have a good friend who has been in the Foreign Office for some years and he tells me the following:—Trotsky arrived at the Foreign Office (State Department) one morning and announced that he was the new Minister for Foreign Affairs; as he does not look like one, everybody laughed; then he felt he must make them a speech to preserve his dignity, which he did. Upon the conclusion of the speech everyone except the messengers who live at the Foreign Office put on his coat and left for home! Another strike!

This is now the sixth day of the revolution, and it is still a success, with no sign of anyone to really combat it. The street fighting now going on is not real opposition; it is mostly for the purpose of instituting and maintaining terror. There is some killing, but apparently what is not deliberate for the purpose of robbery is largely accidental. As heretofore, it is not possible to form a reasonable estimate of the number of dead, but I am convinced it is small. Many of the wounded result from an ignorance of the use of a rifle; workmen with broken jaws have been brought into the hospitals; they did not know the guns would "kick"!

I am promised this will be taken out tomorrow. Now it is late once more and I will say "Spokoiny Nochi" [Good Night] and leave you.

Always affectionately,

No. 8 French Quay,
Petrograd,
November 20, 1917.

My dear—

A friend has promised this will "go out" tomorrow, so I will bring "the situation" up to date.

Each day is considerably like the one before it; street firing is less general, but continues; the weather is vile, with snow frequently; politics are worse than the weather but present nothing as clean looking as snow! Two of our young friends—misses—went to Peter and Paul to see ex-Minister Tereschenko; they were not permitted to see him but were not treated badly. Our Embassy is now working to assist Americans to leave Petrograd and Russia; the Colony grows smaller. There have been several of the Y.W.C.A. and there is much for them to accomplish in Russia.

I hear a great deal of "We must not desert Russia"! That is a very fine sentiment, with which I am in hearty accord, but I have a finer one which reads "We must not desert the United States"!

Walter has talked with a former member of Kerensky's staff, who left Petrograd with Kerensky, and has now returned, in disguise, for a short stay. He stated "Kerensky is now either a prisoner or a fugitive." Just consider for a moment what Kerensky did for Russia; then remember, if you can, what he did for the Allies of Russia; after that don't fail to realize what he did for Germany; a case of misguided judgment! I know of no one man who did more to ruin Russia since my arrival here. I cannot learn that he did anything for the Allies except to balk every move they tried to make. It cannot be denied that Germany has profited to a very great extent indeed by what has taken place in Russia. There is only need to consider the number of divisions Germany has sent from the Russian fronts to Italy and France to be convinced of her gains; the matter of food and other material she has gotten need not be considered unless one wishes to make a list of her gains. I am as certain as I care to be that we will not see Kerensky here anymore; his work is finished.

Last Thursday was my largest "day," in spite of the beastly weather we had, with snow. The number present at one time was forty-one, and nine nations were represented. How very grateful I am for our supply of provisions and how the hot Maryland biscuits with marmalade, did disappear!

A prominent Russian has come to Walter with an appeal to try to save the six ex-Ministers now in Peter and Paul. They are guarded by sailors from Kronstadt, who facetiously joke about the length of time they have to live; the mere mention of Kronstadt sailors is quite enough to make the friends and relatives of those they guard have fears that are justified. Probably they are in danger, but I believe they are as safe in Peter and Paul as they would be any place in Russia, if in prison.

We have been to a large luncheon and dinner party; we gave one of each, also; you will observe that we do not stop meeting people, even if governments do change!

To learn what is going on we *must* meet others; the rumors and reports are boundless; if a person believed *half* what is heard insanity would result.

One of our Russian friends told us of the sad fate of his nephew aged fifteen years, who, with sixty of his fellow military cadets, was murdered; his relatives have heard that his body was thrown into the Moika Canal; they have been unable to find it. Those murdered are frequently thrown into the river or one of the canals; it is another of their habits!

We have met and like tremendously the most attractive Baroness Ixkull,[5] aged seventy, but who looks like, and has the activity, mental and physical, of fifty or less. She has a most interesting home where it will please me to go often to see her wonderful collection of Ikons.

"Smolny" has voted to make Lenin a Dictator! (He was already all of that.) They "vote" there with the readiness with which a hungry horse eats grass! How I wish I could keep or remember all of their "decisions"—one must read them to believe they were made—I have not seen anyone with an imagination extravagant enough to believe what they decide so readily.

Someone objected to the term "menace" I used in connection with the Bolsheviks, and asked, "A menace to what!" My answer was (and will remain) "A menace to civilization; to art; to education; to beauty, morality and to life!" (If I have left out anything you consider important you may add it, because I have not discovered anything attractive in their platform *as it works out*.)

The news from all fronts, brought in by officers escaping from them, simply shows that demoralization and desertion grow daily. Such a large body of men simply could not leave all at once; the number that is leaving causes enough devastation in the country over which they travel. An officer from the Riga Front told me there is now one soldier for every four hundred yards of front. That sounds like a *very* thin line to me and is one of the reasons why the Germans can spare so many divisions for other fronts.

The Executive Committee of the American Lazaret voted today to close the hospital on January first. It was started for "wounded Russian soldiers," of which there will be no more except as a result of fighting amongst themselves. It is now more or less dangerous for the ladies to get there to work, and another of our occupations is cut off! There is continued talk of all foreign women leaving the country but I am not sure that I will be safer en route than am here! I can keep warm here, at least partly warm, and have enough food to last several weeks.

This is certainly a peculiar people; everything is happening yet nothing happens! Everything or nothing can happen to me; as my vote is for "nothing," I am not leaving soon.

---

[5] Vera Ixkull von Hildebrandt was a Baltic German woman who socialized with Americans in Petrograd.

Speaking of voting I forgot to tell you about the suffrage being suddenly given to women here. So far as I can learn it was not asked for by the women, but one morning they woke up to learn that they could vote. Of course no one has really voted for anything since that time everything has been arranged by "decree," but it was both pathetic and amusing when my maid, who is above the average in intelligence and education—she can read and write—tried to learn from me what it really meant "to vote"!

I hear General Kornilov is in good health, though suffering, disheartened, because America cannot help his country. I believe he will be heard from again in Russia, if not soon, then when someone begins to clear the air here.

The American newspaper men here must have their cables censored before they can be sent, so you may readily imagine the only news you get out of Russia is that which the Bolshevik censors think fit to print in the United States. You receive my letters, if at all, from one to two months after they are written, by which time they are ancient history.

Reports from Moscow show the conditions there to be *much* worse than they have been here; more fighting, more looting and burning, more deaths. As conditions here have been bad enough I am glad I am not in Moscow.

Just now we are not sending out our couriers, as the Bolsheviks insist upon the recognition from our Government that is very wisely withheld. To "acknowledge" these villains would be virtual acknowledgment of mob rule, and to agree that *anarchy is a part of the Family of Nations!* Friends offer to take mail for us—we cannot ask them to do so for they certainly jeopardize their own safety by every additional paper they carry which has not the seal of Smolny thereupon. Just at this time no cables are being delivered here and we do not know whether or not those sent really go out; they take them, and the money for them; Walter has received cables that have been here ten days.

I wish I could write in a lighter vein! Sometimes we do forget and joke—but when one starts to write the heavy atmosphere seems to charge. After all, I *am* cheerful, or I would not remain here.

I hesitate to enter the political realm. What I have tried to write you are the facts as I have seen them. There will be many differences of opinion as to how Russia *could* have been saved, but probably no one with knowledge will deny that only *force* could have saved her. There was force in Russia, but it could have been utilized to a better advantage than it was; in fact force brought about the present *mess* (I can think of no more appropriate term) yet it was disorganized (relatively) ignorant force of numbers.

After careful thought I am come to the conclusion that there were *many* causes for the complete downfall of Russia, and I will name some of them:

1. Personal ambition on the part of prominent men in the First Provisional Government.

2. Impractical idealism of other members.
3. Failure of Allies to understand what was brewing and consequent lack of effort to prevent it.
4. National characteristics of educated Russians who saw what was coming but were unable to organize to prevent it.
5. National characteristics of the *un*educated Russians who saw what they *thought* they wanted most and went after it. (Just as a child runs after a toy that has rolled in front of a speeding automobile.)
6. Successful efforts of able German agents to break down Russia's military strength.
7. Opportunities grasped by clever fanatics who also know how to work upon the feelings of the uneducated masses.

Please observe that I begin only with the March Revolution. A book could be written of the things and the people which brought about that revolution, but in April, 1917, Russia was *far* from being ruined. At that time the greatest opportunity to rebuild a most wonderful nation that ever occurred was in Petrograd for the mere asking. The right man, or men, or women, or both, had a chance that will never be repeated!

You see, I am assuming that Russia is now ruined; from my point of view that is the case; I do not mean for all time; the world, and Europe in particular, cannot permit what is going on here to continue indefinitely (and it will get worse before it gets better) any more than the United States can permit one of its central states to maintain a large smallpox camp, with no effort to prevent the spread of the disease. I know that thousands of pages will be written by those brighter than I am upon what has taken place here. Possibly I do not really "know" *all* I state, but there are *some convictions* that closely approach knowledge.

I must now get this into the hands that will try to take it out of Russia. Probably the mere detail of communication difficulties will convince you that "all is not well in Russia"!

Affectionately yours,

French Quay, 8,
Petrograd,
November 29, 1917.

My dear—

This has been a beautiful wintry Thanksgiving Day. The Ambassador gave a reception, but it being my day at home and there being no way to notify the many who always come now that I would not be receiving, I did not go to the Embassy.

There are a few items of interest to "report"; nothing really startling. Smolny has voted to "requisition" whatever private property they need, wherever found, including private deposits in banks, which makes it interesting for those who own furniture and have bank accounts.

We looked from our windows last week and found the Neva full of ice, which forced the steamer, being held in readiness for the escape of the Americans, to be sent to her winter moorings, and that most convenient way out is now closed to us. That merely means it will be more of a scramble when we have to leave, for even if the Germans do not come to Petrograd the food riots sure to come will eventually force us out.

There are many Germans and Austrians here now, ex-prisoners of war, who wander about Petrograd in uniform, quite free and quite safe. The German "assistance" at Smolny seems to be more and more efficient (from a *Hun* point of view), for now we hear nothing of any opposing forces being about to release the tight hold the anarchists have of Petrograd and of Russia!

Before the ice got too thick a Russian cruiser anchored in front of our house and I was in doubt as to whether it was a delicate attention to the French Ambassador next door, or to us! All sailors and ships here now look threatening!

The beautiful residence of our friend in the country has at last been visited in force and the Colonel is in hiding. Two of the servants were killed and many articles of rare worth, including very valuable wines, were taken. A storm has arisen in the politico-military atmosphere; the Military Attaches of the Allies, excepting the American, signed a letter at Army Headquarters, which is by way of being a protest, and almost a threat, on account of the very evident *official* quitting of the Russian armies. To me it seems so useless, since there ceased to be any Russian armies some weeks ago. The Hotel Astoria was again "searched" last night, for no apparent reason. It rather looks like that devoted place is searched for the amusement of the searchers! Every so often a group of guards who have not had the pleasure of turning out and threatening ladies and gentlemen at two or three o'clock in the morning start a search, and the nominal government status of that hotel makes it the easiest prey, though of course other places are "searched." A few nights before this last revolution the Provisional Government sent guards of Junkers to protect some of the Allied Embassies; as soon as the revolution was a success the Embassies were protecting the Junkers! At the French Embassy Junkers were on guard at the front door, while a Bolshevik guard looked after the rear entrance.

The seriousness prevents one from laughing at such a situation, but the fine young Military Cadets are to be pitied; they are only boys, keen to do their duty, and many have been needlessly murdered. They have been leaving our Embassy singly, sometimes in disguise, as safe opportunity offered. Think of it! Here are 180,000,000 people with no government! A certain *power*, in this ex-capital, and to a less extent in other places, is attempting to control, but lack of education, coupled with desires we call insane, prevent organized government, and all is running wild. I have talked with Americans who were in Moscow when the revolution broke there; they lived in the cellar of the Hotel Metropole for three days, subsisting on potato soup! The hotel over their heads was demolished by gunfire during that time. People began the old custom of shooting from the windows, and a veritable civil war ensued. At present Russians do not hesitate to kill Russians; they believe it wrong, very wrong, to kill Germans!

The disregard of foreigners and foreign diplomats has begun to break out; the Belgian Minister and his wife were forced to get out of their automobile and walk home while their car was "commandeered" by the anarchists. The Belgian flag was in evidence on the auto and the Minister showed his passport, but that did not make any difference. "No more diplomats!" "All internationalists!" "No more private automobiles; all public property!" Those were the answers the Minister received to his protests, and then he walked.

Walter has been trying very hard to get a plan of his accepted which will accomplish a real government here.

December fifth.

It has not been possible to send this away but tomorrow it is leaving for home. Nothing of importance has happened. The few simple social functions continue and we have been to the theater, opera and ballet, all of which I enjoy thoroughly. The Neva is now frozen over solid and gives us a large plain of snow in front of our house. Some of the views, particularly at sunset, beggar description. The Prison and Fortress, Peter and Paul, is near us on the opposite shore and plainly visible from our windows. We received an advance Christmas present in the shape of some maple sugar from a friend in Chicago, and you may suspect how it appeals to us in this sweetless land!

A general strike, to include all railroads and industries, is promised us for tomorrow; there is really no object in these strikes except the one desired by Berlin, and prohibitive wages are now being paid; any increase will only destroy more industries. The purchasing value of a ruble is so small that comparisons with former prices are beyond the arithmetical capacity of my brain. I simply know that I would rather walk than to pay forty rubles (about $4.00 in our money just now) to ride in an ezevoschick for fifteen minutes!

I have seen the wonderful Karsavina[6] dance a ballet, and now I do not believe I can ever see better dancing. Possibly her wonderful art made the music seem superior —at any rate I can have no regrets at missing the best that Russia (the world!) affords. How sorry I am that could not have seen Russia in the days of her plenty and safety! From all I can learn I would never have been shocked by the treatment of the work-

---

[6] Tamara Karsavina (1885–1978) was a ballerina of the Imperial Russian Ballet and the Ballets Russes.

ing classes, who, as nearly as I can gather, were to be most favorably compared, as regards necessities and comforts, with all others of their class in the world. Of course, there was practically no political freedom, and cruel measures were sometimes taken to suppress, control and punish political offenders. From the results I have seen accomplished by these same offenders, I am of the opinion the measures were not quite complete. We do not have political freedom in our primary schools, nor in our lunatic asylums, and certainly the brains of these people in the Bolshevik ranks may be classed with those which are found in either of the two institutions named.

In general the news is:—Petrograd is still here; a part of Moscow is no longer there; many handsome estates are no longer anywhere; the Bolsheviks are everywhere. To fully understand conditions in Russia one must live here and endeavor to "keep house"; no language can make conditions clear to those who do not know Russia, and those who do know it, but have not been here for some months, would have great difficulty in really comprehending what is going on now.

I must get this ready for the mail. Love from both to all.

French Quay, 8,
Petrograd,
December 15, 1917.

My dear—

Real Russian Winter we have been having; cold, raw, dark and gloomy, with wind and snow! That makes it so cheerful, with politics and weather alike, to say nothing of the increasing number of murders and robberies, and the constant rifle shots one hears, sometimes without leaving home. We got up early one morning to say goodbye at the Finland Station to some Americans who were leaving, and the light effects at sunrise were something wonderful. I shall not get up that early often, it is not done in Petrograd, but I have another everlasting pleasant memory of Russia.

Again we have been out to luncheons, dinners, theater and ballet, but I always sigh with relief when I get home safely. We have given two dinner parties since I last wrote you, one of them for nine American men; women are getting scarce here. We saw a very interesting play which had only been given once before; that time in the Winter Palace, when several of the Grand Dukes, including Constantine,[7] who wrote the play, took part. The beautiful costumes and scenery were recently unearthed in some of the searches and the play put on.

Some soldiers and workmen have robbed the wine cellars of the Winter Palace, and the air for two or three blocks around the Palace is redolent with the fumes of the superior wines; the snow is stained and covered with broken bottles. They carried

---

[7] Grand Duke Konstantin Konstantinovich (1858–1915) was a member of the royal family, grandson of Tsar Nicholas I.

away much of the wine and friends have told me they have purchased from the soldiers some fine old vintage for a song, but I am not brave enough to buy wine from a drunken soldier or sailor! Many food and wine shops have been similarly looted and wrecked, it being the practice to approach a shop in a motor truck, with rifles and machine guns popping. That drives all in the neighborhood indoors or away, and the fun begins; the shooting is kept up by a part of the crowd, in order to keep the streets cleared. A great deal is consumed on the spot; a very small amount is carried away—for the powers in Smolny do not permit anything to be carried away from such parties—and the remainder is destroyed. Broken bottles and wine stains in the snow remain in evidence until the next fall of snow covers them. When we walked past the Winter Palace after the "party" there the *fire engine*, with streams from which the looters had been driven from the cellars, was still standing there. It is reported that some of the drunken ones were drowned in the cellars. I saw the bars broken from the cellar windows and many guards standing about. This is another case of locking the stable door after the horse has been stolen, but is one of many. The horrible things all happen, then Smolny makes any effort to show how good they are! They may fool some people.

Just now there is a scandal at Smolny; a certain Lieutenant Schnaur was made Bolshevik Chief of Staff. His dealings with the Germans became too open and bold, and Smolny, in a fit of righteous indignation, arrested and confined him. He will not be punished! Observe that Smolny is clever; the Bolsheviks are certainly in close touch and accord with the Germans, yet they make a great noise when one man is so careless as to let everybody know that he is working for the Germans! By special arrangement we attended a tea where the Bolshevik Commander of the Winter Palace was present. He calls himself Pokrovsky and is high in Bolshevik councils.

Russian officers are coming in increasing numbers to make arrangements to join the American forces in France or the United States. Many of them appeal to me to intercede with Walter when I meet them at other homes; they are very loath to take "no" for an answer! A warm hearted Russian lady who is, I am sure, deep in the counter-revolutionary movement, has warned Walter that he is to be accused by the Bolsheviks of dealing in Russian political affairs. As he has positively refused to have anything to do with such matters, and will so continue, any such accusation will be without foundation in fact. Possibly because so many Russian officers come to this apartment they think he *must* be plotting! Probably my Thursday afternoons, now always very largely attended, add to the suspicion. I hope they *do* annoy the Bolsheviks, for they make many others warm and happy and they are as innocent as if you were giving them—only—we learn a great deal from those who come in!

Today two Russian officers were walking along the crowded Nevsky in uniform; they were set upon by some soldiers, badly beaten, robbed, and their marks of rank torn off. The large crowd did not interfere. As Walter was returning from the Embassy today a soldier standing quite near fired his rifle. We think he did it to see him jump, which he did not do, but he *did* watch that soldier out of the corner of his eye to see if he would take aim for another shot!

We are working hard now to close the Lazaret; we have considerable of hospital supplies and clothing, for which there is great need, and which we will distribute to worthy places. The Salvation Army does much good here in an unobtrusive way and we will give them a large share of our supplies.

There is still much talk of a German Army coming here, but I believe they will wait until the weather is more settled and the ground more solidly frozen. There *is* an army of Germans here now, but not organized as such. We live near the ex-Austrian Embassy; we see Germans and Austrians in uniform entering and leaving it. Germany is getting considerable of "aid and comfort" from Russia, which either makes Bolshevik Russia an ally of Germany or a traitor to the Allies; it matters not what one calls it; in my opinion all one hears about how the Bolsheviks detest the Germans and the German Autocracy is German-made noise to create an impression.

We have been informed that hereafter all rent must be paid to the Bolsheviks; as we owe our rent to a gentleman in the United States it will not be paid until it can be paid to him; we cannot deposit funds to his credit in the banks here—it would be as wise to deposit it in the Neva—the banks are gradually ceasing to bank!

We are having great difficulty in keeping warm. The majolica tile stoves look very well, and sometimes we can get them quite warm, but they will not heat all of Russia and our apartment is now surrounded by atmosphere and uninhabited apartments. The Kadet Club once occupied the floor above us; that has been closed and sealed as being counter-revolutionary; the Russians living under us did not return for the winter. By burning a great deal of wood and all our lamps we keep very comfortable, but when the wood and kerosene we now have are gone we will not get any more, and we *must* look ahead.

The threatened decree abolishing all officers except those "elected" by the men has gone into effect; a Russian officer told me that a friend of his, a Colonel, is now one of the *cooks* in his *own* regiment.

We received a paper directing us to supply the two warm articles of clothing of which I have told you, or two blankets; Walter declined to contribute; we are wondering what the next move will be! Friends tell us they have seen articles supplied in accordance with that decree for sale in the Thieves' Market, and I believe it; I have seen great sleigh loads of the "contributions" on the streets.

Trotsky's latest speech contains a cheerful reference to "a machine the French Revolution produced which reduced the length of a man by the length of his head"; simultaneously appeared in a newspaper a description of an electrical invention by a Russian which would instantly behead many people at the same time! *So*—you see we are getting on! Trotsky, in his speech, only suggested that the Bolsheviks had not yet begun to behead all well-dressed people by wholesale, but they had it in mind and would not forget the possibilities. However, I remain hopeful, and I am not alarmed, which does not seem at all right. I really should be scared and run away, but I have a real desire to remain indefinitely! I want to see this thing out, but my best friends tell me I won't live long enough even if I go home to see Russia settled, and if I stay here I will not live very long!

At any rate, I am still very much alive and send you much love.

8 French Quay,
Petrograd,
December 24, 1917.

My dear—

Christmas Eve, but how very little like it! We had some friends here for luncheon today and called at two of the Legations this afternoon; that is the extent of our celebration, though we are all going to a dance at the National City Bank tomorrow night, which has been arranged by Mrs. Walter Farwell,[8] an enthusiastic American who still remains in Petrograd. It's a huge undertaking in such times as this.

Two of our Russian friends have received visits from the "search" parties: Riabova, one of the handsome estates we visited, and the apartment of a dear friend in town. My friend's husband was out of town and the brutes were *eight hours* searching her apartment and cellar. She tells me she was too angry to be frightened.

Last Monday we awoke to the realization that all switzars (doorkeepers) and dvorniks (janitors) in the city were on a strike, the same having been ordered by Smolny. Our dear old switzar is very sad—he does not want to strike; he is threatened with death if he works![9] The annoying part of it was that we were giving a dinner on Monday night and the front door was locked; the owner was afraid to open it. Our guests had to come in the back way, through the kitchen! The dvorniks bring up the daily supply of wood. The cook told me we could have no meals. Walter said he would carry up wood; cook said dvorniks would not permit. Walter told her she should look out of the window and see an interesting murder if the dvorniks tried to prevent him from carrying his own wood to his own kitchen! The dvorniks came out and watched him at work, but they also watched a convenient club he had carefully tested and laid on the snow within easy reach, but they did not interfere! He carried up enough for three days and the dvornik strike was over at the end of that time, but not so with the switzars. Before Thursday we had obtained a key from the owner and stationed one maid at the front door, with orders to admit anyone who stated they wished to call upon us. This is all part of the effort to make the "bourgeoisie" uncomfortable, and

---

[8] Mildred Farwell (1880?–1941) was a correspondent for the *Chicago Times* and was married to a member of the Red Cross Mission, Walter Farwell.

[9] Crosley is a little confused here. The *switzsar* was a guard. The *dvornik* was a doorman who also performed some janitorial duties and might have looked after such matters as firewood.

it succeeded very well while the strike lasted. I believe the wages of those who struck have been increased about seven hundred per cent!

I have heard the wonderful Schalyapin,[10] who refuses to sing any more at Marinsky Theater[11] but appears only at Narodny Dom[12] (People's House), in the Opera, Boris Godunov,[13] and now I believe I have seen and heard the best Russia has on the stage, but I wish I could see much more of it.

Whenever we go out we hear firing, but we have been fortunate in being able to avoid the immediate vicinity of bullets. I wonder how long our good luck will last!

There is considerable of a tempest against Americans being stirred up just now, and it was brought to a climax by the arrest and confinement in Peter and Paul of our friend Colonel Kalpaschnikov, who was once a secretary of the Russian Embassy in Washington; he spent some time in the United States during the war lecturing in the interests of the Russian Red Cross and took back to Russia considerable Red Cross supplies, including many automobiles, as the result of his lectures and contributions in the United States. He was detailed to assist the American Red Cross Mission to Rumania, but the Bolsheviks accused the American Ambassador and Colonel Kalpashnikov of plotting against them and in favor of the Cossacks.[14] The Colonel is in prison and the newspapers are full of the ridiculous accusations against our Ambassador. I will give you a translation of one of the articles, which is, of course, quite untrue:

---

[10] Fyodor Shaliapin (1873–1938) was an internationally known Russian opera singer, famous especially for his lead role in the opera "Boris Godunov." He died of leukemia in 1938.

[11] The Mariinsky Theater in St. Petersburg has been a premiere venue for opera and ballet since the middle of the nineteenth century.

[12] "Narodny Dom" literally means "People's House," and was a cultural and leisure center where individuals could visit a library and attend lectures, performances, and meetings.

[13] Boris Godunov (1551–1605) was a nobleman at the court of Ivan the Terrible. His sister married Ivan's son, the feeble-minded and sickly Fyodor, and when Ivan died, Godunov became the de facto regent for the new tsar. When Tsar Fyodor died in 1598, Godunov ruled Russia until his own death in 1605. Modest Mussorgsky, the Russian composer, wrote an opera titled *Boris Godunov* in 1868–69.

[14] Crosley has described the scandal surrounding Colonel Andrei Kalpashnikov accurately. Kalpashnikov had raised enough money in the United States to purchase seventy-two ambulances and eight other vehicles, which were shipped semi-assembled to Petrograd in 1917. He and his vehicles, however, became caught up in the rapidly changing political situation in Russia and he was arrested by the new Bolshevik government and imprisoned for five months; when he was released, he fled the country using false papers.

A COMPLOT FOR THE IMPERIALISTS WITH GENERAL KALEDIN[15]

Several Allied Officers and members of the Allied Missions and Embassies have allowed themselves to mix actively in the internal life of Russia, and of course they are not on the side of the people, but on the side of the Counter-Revolutionary-Imperialistic Kaledin-Kadet-Party.

We have warned these busy persons several times but the hour has apparently arrived for the last warning. The most important of the representatives of the United States are involved in the Kaledin Complot.

They took every means to support him, under cover of the Red Cross designated for the South-West Front; the American officers in Jassy, Anderson[16] and Perkins,[17] and their co-workers, the Russian Officers Kalpashnikov and Verblunsky,[18] made an attempt to deceive the vigilance of the authorities of the Council, and to send several automobiles and many other things, to the Don, for the use of Kaledin.

The complot has been discovered; Kalpashnikov and the others who took part have been arrested; papers of considerable importance have been seized. In the telegram from Mr. Anderson, the Chief of the American Red Cross Mission in Jassy, Colonel Kalpashnikov has been directed to receive from Mr. Francis, the Ambassador of the United States, 100,000 rubles for the delivery of a train to Rostov on the Don!

In the papers signed by Mr. Francis is a certificate that the train is going "from Petrograd to Jassy"! Now the mysterious train will go nowhere; it is detained in Petrograd by the power of the Council.

The complot is discovered, the complot of the Americans (and not only the Americans) Imperialists with Kaledin. The threads of the complot lead, as we saw they would, to very high places. The next word should be from Mr. Francis and from those who sent him here.

---

[15] Aleksei Kaledin (1861–1918) was a Don Cossack officer who opposed the Bolshevik Revolution and attempted to assert control of the Don region until the power of the Provisional Government had been restored. When his followers decided to surrender to the Bolshevik forces, he committed suicide in February 1918.

[16] Henry Watkins Anderson (1870–1954) was chief of the American Red Cross Mission in Romania in 1917.

[17] Roger Perkins (1874–1936) was a doctor who participated in the American Red Cross Mission in Romania.

[18] Verblunsky was an assistant of Anderson, of the Red Cross.

The foregoing is only one of many articles that have appeared in the papers, the Ambassador having caused to be printed a very dignified statement to the effect that the accusations were false. As a matter of fact, Smolny did not print *all* the papers taken at Colonel Kalpashnikov's apartment; if they had done so even a child could have seen that there was nothing in the charges.

The times are really strenuous and it is difficult to collect one's wits sufficiently to write a connected account of all that takes place. No sooner do the details of one startling event become known than another more startling bursts forth, and so it will continue. We now live from day to day, questioning what Russia and Petrograd has in store for us. "Do you think the Germans will come here?" "When do you think the Germans will reach Petrograd?" "What will you do when the Germans get here!" are all samples of questions now being asked us constantly. Our thoughts and conversations are empty of all save the terrible calamities of Russia. Can my attention ever be fixed on other subjects? The Russians seem as mystified as the strangers within their gates at all the irregularities of the present political powers, the queer decrees and demands made by each new party-power!

The Lenin-Trotsky combination is a joke and a sad reality at the same time. There are many ideas among the Russians as to how the evils should be corrected, but there the subject ends. When a people arise in their own midst, make new laws of their own fancy, and disregard all past accepted ones, it is somewhat astounding, don't you think?

The soldiers, or some in soldiers' uniforms, are, from day to day, breaking into wine shops and drinking all they want—can't you see them? Some get home and others get shot, while others fall asleep in the snow. We are getting accustomed to these "peculiarities"; a bit unsafe, perhaps, to be on the street at such moments as a stray bullet might hit the wrong person—but we go out, and even get home quite late.

An exceedingly clever young Russian officer who was recently at dinner here explained why he had not come to see me on Thursday, as he had intended doing. When quite near, on his way here, in broad daylight, some men attempted to relieve him of his warm fur coat; the officer gave one of the brutes a blow that sent him reeling; his resistance (a *very* unusual thing since death was the price of the slightest resistance as the attackers were usually three to one and armed with bayonets) surprised the remainder very much and they let him alone, but he feared if he came here they might follow him into our apartment, so he went in the opposite direction.

We gave a dinner of fifteen, with five nations represented at the table; everything on the table except three vegetables came from New York. A Russian Colonel said to his daughter: "It is like a Little America!"

We now have our dress suit cases packed with our warmest clothing and Walter has studied all available routes of escape. If the Germans do come he has no intention of being captured! I smile as I write that, for it is quite possible that we will not have to run, nor be permitted to run! Some of the weather we have been having would quite prevent a flight.

I was quite touched while calling on the sad and wistful Baroness Pahlen [?], who went to a secret drawer in a desk, removed a beautiful old red lacquer box—and gave it to me. All her ancestors were Cossacks; her family always occupied high places at Court, before the revolution; she is sweet, womanly and devoutly religious.

One of the latest decrees announces the "requisition" of all private funds in the banks, in accordance with previous threats; we are removing ours gradually, but please do not tell anyone!

The Russians are saying: "We found the Czar was bad; we got rid of him!" "We learned the Provisional Government was bad; we got rid of that!" "We see the Bolsheviks are bad!" "Who is good and what can we do?" Isn't it all a sad mix-up!

This letter is long enough; I will write again in a few days; I am going to have a letter always ready to send out if opportunity offers. Good night!

Affectionately,

8 French Quay,
Petrograd,
December 28, 1917.

My dear—

The last letter has left, via Siberia, so I will get another ready.

Christmas Day was hardly different from other days! I received some lovely flowers, which quite fill my room, and there were callers, but no one feels as they like to feel at this season. The dance and supper at the National City Bank was a great success—so many people had such a good time. It was the happiest gathering I have seen in Petrograd; mostly Americans there, with a few of their most intimate Russian friends, and some English officers.

I wrote you of the fine young brother of my little interpreter friend, who went to the Riga Front in the artillery. His men ordered him to clean their horses. He escaped and is here on "sick leave."

Various people have called to request our assistance in getting Colonel Kalpashnikov out of Peter and Paul. It is not possible for us to help him, in view of the false accusations that have been made against the American Embassy, but I have sent him articles of food he cannot get otherwise. The American Manager of the National City Bank was arrested and marched through the streets, his only crime consisting in being a bank manager! They only kept him prisoner for a few hours, but the bank remains closed. He called on me that same afternoon, and, in spite of his great responsibility, he is very calm about it all.

We are now informed the water supply will be cut off, so we keep bath tub and all other available containers full of water. The pipes will freeze if the water is really turned off, and then we *will* be in a predicament. We are hoping it is only another threat, but these "Reds" have a way of carrying out their threats! We learn there are two American couriers, with sixteen bags of mail, being held at Torneo,[19] in the north of Finland; that is the Christmas mail for which we have been longing. It is only another detail to show their power and their delight at making some others unhappy.

Peace pourparlers[20] between the Bolsheviks and the Germans now have the stage. The Constituent Assembly has again come to the front, but those members believed to be antagonistic to the Bolsheviks were arrested *as they arrived* in Petrograd and my conclusion of some weeks ago that the Assembly would not meet is confirmed. The number of uniformed Germans seen in the streets is increasing and one cannot go out without seeing some of them. Quarters have been prepared for a German Delegation to occupy. I wish I felt as safe here as I feel the Germans will be!

To show how the respect for foreigners has disappeared I give you the following items, in addition to the holding up of our couriers with mail: The apartment of the First Secretary of the Italian Embassy was looted and furniture smashed. Ten mail pouches for the British Embassy are missing. The Spanish courier trying to enter Russia (Finland) at Torneo was not permitted to enter because he did not have the visée of the Russian "Commissaire" at Stockholm. Another meeting of protest against Americans and their treatment of anarchists in the United States was held. A committee of four anarchists called at the American Embassy to present threats about killing Americans in Petrograd.

We tried for some time one morning to get a number on the telephone; finally I told the maid, who was then trying, to speak in German. She was frightened, but finally did so, and immediately got the number we desired; she also was thanked by the operator for using German!

We have been offered a number of palaces and handsome apartments rent free, merely if we will occupy them for protection. The Russian owners are badly unnerved and do not realize that foreigners are *not* a protection now. We will not move from this apartment until we move from Petrograd, for I do not believe our American friends from whom we have it will return to Russia under existing conditions. It will make me very sad to be obliged to leave all these beautiful things to the mercies of hoodlums, not to mention the stores of expensive provisions belonging to us.

There was recently a farce of an election for *another* Constitutional Assembly; ballot boxes were taken to Peter and Paul and the prisoners there, including the Ministers of the Provisional Government, were permitted to vote. Of course the Bolsheviks counted the votes, so it is quite natural they should have received a majority vote, as

---

[19] Torneo was a rail customs border point on the Russian (Finnish)-Swedish border, the only way into the West because of German control of the seas. It was the route used by Lenin, Trotsky, and many Americans.

[20] *Pourparlers* is French for "negotiations."

had been expected, but still I believe no Assembly will meet. Such an Assembly *might* form a real government and the Lenin-Trotsky combination does not wish a real government here anymore than Germany does. If it does meet, and attempts to draw up a Bolshevik-Anarchist Constitution, it will fail, because there are now three distinct groups with different interests, namely, the (so-called) soldiers, the workmen, and the peasants. Each peasant is willing to have more land than he now owns; he is unwilling to give a part of his land to another who has less, or to give all his land to "Smolny"; that last does not appeal to him at all!

The workmen are receiving relatively enormous wages as members of the Red Guard, which they do not wish to relinquish any more than they wish to return to work. The soldiers see the Red Guard receiving more pay than they get; that annoys them. So the way is not yet smooth for the establishment of an ideal "Socialistic-Revolutionary-Republic," whatever that is! There will still be many troubles to overcome and things to learn before Petrograd or any part of Russia, is even peaceful, not to mention a real government.

I wonder if you read of the Russian "Committee" that first visited the German Headquarters to talk peace! A lieutenant with a bad record, an army Doctor and a soldier were "elected" to go to the German lines! The whole peace negotiations have been so disgusting that I have said but little about them. It is disgusting to think the Germans believe they are really fooling anyone with intelligence! It is not so surprising that these dark minds should believe they are fooling the "Intelligentsia."

Our electric light situation is now a serious matter; the current is cut off unexpectedly at any time, and we never know when we will have it; it is a great nuisance. Our candles still hold out (we bought all we could find) and our kerosene stoves and lamps are a great comfort.

No more this time! I will write again as soon as this leaves. No need to worry about us. *We* are quite well and propose to take good care of ourselves.

With best love to you all,

8 French Quay,
Petrograd,
January 3, 1918.

My dear—

There isn't much to tell you, but I am going to continue my efforts to have a letter always ready to send. Chances to send letters will be more rare from now on, but probably items of real interest will be the same, so you lose nothing!

We finally received our Christmas mail and it furnished almost a real belated Christmas for us; there were many letters, some presents and a great deal of good news from those we love most.

Street demonstrations and parades have begun anew here, with banners tending to strike terror to the hearts of all who love law and order. As nearly as I can determine, these fiends wish everything "downed," and nothing but their own powers elevated. All their banners begin "Down with—"! Murders of the most respected men in Russia are reported daily from all over the country, and the press here now would make the most yellow journal you ever saw look like a Sunday School Weekly!

We have experienced a Petrograd fog, a real one. We had a dinner engagement at the home of the British Chaplain and started in an ezevoschick in plenty of time to arrive for dinner. After two *very* narrow escapes from collisions I decided to walk, but only by keeping close to the walls of the buildings could we find our way. We were late for dinner and had to walk home, but thereby obtained our exercise.

The Ambassador gave a reception at the Embassy on January first where we again met the fast dwindling American Colony, as well as some Russians. That list grows smaller, also, for all Russians who believe they have a safe place to go to are leaving Petrograd. Many find that the place they select is safe on the day of their arrival but becomes unsafe the next day.

I received a telephone call asking me to visit Baroness K—, who is ill, and who had a letter for Walter from Colonel Kalpashnikov. I went, and can't get over the sadness the plight of that family caused me. The Baron is an officer whose pay is five rubles per month; that is about five cents in our money, so far as its purchasing value is concerned. The sweet wife has obtained a temporary position in an office, at a salary of 175 rubles per month, which will not pay their rent. They have two small children, also, which makes the case more sad. Of course that is only one family—there are thousands in similar circumstances.

The "letter" from Colonel Kalpashnikov was on a small strip of paper which had been smuggled out of the prison and read:

> **DEAR CAPTAIN CROSLEY:** Many thanks for the books, the excellent bread and the jam. The food we get is very bad and especially in very small portions, and your kind attentions help to keep up my life in jail. Conditions are every day getting darker and all my hope to get out soon is in your hands. Please thank Mrs. Crosley for the bread and, believe me, most truly yours,
>
> "A. KALPASHNIKOV."

This is one of several similar letters he has been able to smuggle out, and I have sent him several packages of provisions. Some, of course, he will not receive, but whatever he does get will make life easier for him.

Today we had a real blizzard, but many callers braved the storm and I was so glad I had made preparations for them. Our cheerful open fires and candle-light, aided by screened lamps, make the rooms look very pretty and all enjoy them so. One dear Russian lady said, "Why—it is a bit of fairyland!" They show they enjoy it by staying very late, and generally some stay for dinner.

There really is nothing *new* to relate—it is the same old story, with Russia getting darker and deeper in the mire of anarchy and hunger and grief each day. The point is that *everything*, without an exception, grows worse and nothing gets better. Russians and others without food are starving; we are very fortunate in having our provisions, which we hope to keep until *we* use them. Walter is still working hard to prevent the Huns from owning Russia, or a part of it. If decisive steps could only be taken! The Germans swagger about Petrograd as if they already own it. German Commissions are here, with large staffs, and also many German businessmen. It is disgusting as well as discouraging! I find it grows more difficult to write letters; new things do not happen; only more of the old ones. We are well and in good spirits, in spite of disagreeable surroundings.

Yours always,

French Quay, 8,
Petrograd,
January 10, 1918.

My dear—

This will be my busy day, for there will be many callers, as now happens every Thursday, and tonight we go to the Chinese Legation. The Chinese Minister and his wife are dears, and we are particularly fond of one of the Secretaries. We have had more blizzard weather and we suffer from the cold, despite the large quantities of wood we burn. When we have guests I manage to get the apartment fairly comfortable, but we can't burn wood at the rate that requires every day! We concentrate on one room, ordinarily, and carry a kerosene stove to one in use only for a time. We have had again two dinners of sixteen guests at each and have been out twice. It is a very great pleasure to entertain, for I am able to give my friends so many things they cannot get elsewhere.

Russian Christmas has come and gone; we went to two churches to hear the wonderful mixed choirs sing. I have never before heard such harmony. A special effort is made to have the Christmas choirs particularly effective. We went with Captain and Mrs. Egorev to the Admiralty Church. One of the priests, or "deacons," had such a strong, deep and melodious voice. There is no organ or other musical accompaniment in the churches. This man was very large and handsome, as well, and the service was very impressive. Unfortunately the decline of the church keeps pace with other degradations, and I fear will not recover soon.

Nearly all members of the crews of the British submarines in the Baltic have been sent home, it being evident that those submarines cannot accomplish anything against the Russians *and* the Germans. Of course the ice prevents them from operating now, and to have the men here in the spring would only subject them to loss of life, for it now seems apparent the Allies will not send an armed force here soon enough to be of any service in retaining a part of the Russian armies on the front.

We went Christmas shopping alone to get presents for some Russian children, and found a shop where they were so glad we could speak German! It made it easier for us to buy toys, but we were somewhat embarrassed to buy in that language.

The latest horror is the murder of a large number of officers at Sevastopol, under particularly disgusting conditions. This is the first wholesale murder that has been committed for some time, and shows that affairs are getting worse.

We have about five hours of electric light per day now, though we may not count upon that. It is "daylight" from nine in the morning till three in the afternoon, but much of that daylight is quite dark. We would be lost without our lamps and candles. We must nurse them, but *they* will not ring the doorbell. We try to keep a maid near the front door to hear the pounding, but the kitchen is *so* much warmer!

Smolny has issued an allegorical poster, of which I will send you a copy, with a translation attached. I purposely leave the translation in the original form; it is rather unique language. Please note that the poster carries out my expressed belief that destruction is what is sought. Russia is a wonderful country, full of lights and shadows, though just now the shadows have the advantage. It is too bad that the world must lose so much that was beautiful in Russia to receive—what? Something much worse than nothing!

We are still living from day to day; no plans for the future are possible. I am sure we shall have to leave eventually, but whether we will be forced out by Germans or Russians no one knows. Please don't worry about us; some of the letters we receive indicate that some of you have not the confidence in us that we have! It is much more likely that we shall be safe than otherwise. Remember, we will not starve! With love and regards to all,

Affectionately,

No. 8 French Quay,
Petrograd,
January 20, 1918.

My dear—

Considerable has happened in the past ten days, but it has all been of the same sort as before and all leading down, not upward! We have had very cold weather, with considerable snow, and less electric light. We have continued to go out at night, but very few of our friends are doing it. It is the only way to know what goes on at night and Walter considers it very important to know. We have closed the Lazaret, for its usefulness had ceased.

The Rumanian Minister and his entire staff were arrested by the Bolsheviks because of clashes between the Rumanian Army and the Bolsheviks who were trying to contaminate it. They were kept in Peter and Paul for three days, being released after a protest was made by the Diplomatic Corps. It is reported they are to be given their passports and escorted out of Russia!

One day we managed to get our bedroom heated to sixty-four degrees Fahrenheit by the use of the wood stove and two kerosene stoves, all at the same time. That, of course, is too extravagant to be considered as a regular thing. We simply did it to see how warm we *could* make that room.

The crowds, the looting, the shooting and the murders on the streets have increased greatly, and now bombs are being used—just why all of this has broken out anew no one seems to know, unless it is a part of the progressive destruction already planned. Hunger and cold are no doubt responsible for some of it, and most likely the nature of the beast makes the remainder easy. There is no organized opposition against the Bolsheviks and there are no fights between bodies of men. The shooting and other terrorism is being carried out by small bands, and more innocent people are killed than of the other sort. A well-dressed man was wounded on the street near here; a Red Cross Nurse, in uniform, attempted to assist him; she was bayoneted for so doing. A young soldier tried to aid the nurse; he was attacked and wounded! Can you imagine the frame of mind that permits—nay, *encourages*—all this!

A threat has been made to bomb and burn the American Embassy tonight, but it won't be done. If the anarchists really want to do that they will not let us know about it beforehand. Probably the most dastardly crime of all was committed last night in the Marie Hospital. Ministers Shingarov,[21] and Kokochkine,[22] of the last Provisional Government, were arrested on November seventh in the Winter Palace and imprisoned in Peter and Paul. They became quite ill and were removed to the hospital. Last night they were murdered in their beds by a group of men in uniform! No one will even be arrested for that crime. My friend Baroness Maydell took an ezevoschick to do some shopping; she kept it waiting in front of a shop. When she came out the driver fussed about being kept waiting. A rough crowd immediately gathered with cries of "Throw her in the Neva!" Do such details bore you? What else is there to write

---

[21] Andrei I. Shingarev (1869–1918) was a member of the Kadet Party in the Duma and served as minister of agriculture, then minister of finance, under the Provisional Government. He was arrested by the Bolsheviks in late 1917 and imprisoned in the Peter Paul Fortress. He was later murdered by Bolshevik sailors in January 1918 after being transferred to a hospital due to illness.

[22] Fyodor F. Kokoshkin (1871–1918) was a member of the Kadet Party and served as controller in the Provisional Government. He was arrested by the Bolsheviks in late 1917 and imprisoned in the Peter Paul Fortress. Along with Shingarev, he was later murdered by Bolshevik sailors in January 1918 after being transferred to a hospital due to illness.

about? The murders of officers at Sevastopol have been repeated and an officer from there told me that seventy have been killed recently. Why? Who knows?

Walter assures me I have been a very great help to him here, so I am very glad I came with him. It is reasonable to assume that a handsome apartment with a hostess would draw a larger group than a widower's hall, and Walter insists that the friends I have helped him to make have been more than worth the effort. Therefore, as I am not *yet* frightened, I remain on, though strongly advised to go.

The American couriers have not been permitted to leave for some time now, and several of them are here. How favorably they compare with the Russians, and how proud I am of them! *Why* couldn't we have had five hundred of them here three months ago and avoided this horrible mess? The dislike for and disregard of foreigners is on the increase; the Italian Embassy was recently violated and something stolen. Just now there is an evident effort to drive foreigners out, but it is worthy of note that the targets for the insults are the Allies and not the Neutrals, which indicates German-make! This belief is given additional strength by the ever-increasing numbers of German and Austrian soldiers and officers seen on the streets. Many of them are ex-prisoners of war, now quite free, but others have been recognized by Russian officers who knew them before the war began.

Our own plight here is bad enough, but that of the educated Russians is infinitely worse; they see their fortunes and estates taken, their own lives in danger, their loved ones suffering from cold and hunger, and they can do nothing. While an equal number of Americans *would* "do something," we cannot blame these people for the system under which they were brought up and educated, nor for the characteristics that system has developed in them. While no normal mind would believe that system to be wholly good, no one with such a mind who has lived here and seen what I have seen can believe it is being improved upon now! If there was "graft" before, what has taken its place is infinitely worse.

I have seen considerable of Russia, and have talked with many intelligent Russians who know their country; it is *not* a *characteristic* of the educated Russian that he spares himself, he will take all blame to which he is entitled, and more.

I went to a Russian New Year's Eve party! Now it is late again and I must leave you. *How* I would love to see you all! I will some day, and it will be a happy reunion.

Always faithfully yours,

French Quay, 8,
Petrograd,
January 31, 1918.

My dear—

This letter must confirm only what has appeared in my other letters. I cannot make these people change their habits nor make history that won't make! There has positively been nothing to happen but more of "the same," and the result is that life grows more gloomy, yet at the same time more "peppery."

The weather has been bad, alternately thawing and freezing, with a resulting frightful condition of the streets, which of course have not been cleared of snow this year, because that means work. But the Bolsheviks have now ordered that *everybody* (except soldiers and workmen) must work in the streets, and one sees officers in uniform, ladies in sealskin coats, and children working with pick and shovel, removing snow from the streets. Of course they do not receive pay! While they are working some soldiers and workmen line up on the sidewalks and stare at them with a vague expression.

We have given two more large dinners, and have been out several times, but it is becoming a great effort to entertain *or* to be entertained. The streets are really not safe, and no one enjoys going out at night. I love the excitement of it, but am glad to get home in safety each time.

Robbers are now stripping people of their clothes on the streets; one couple was left quite naked on a bitter cold night; they were taken into the apartment occupied by some of our friends, so I know it to be true. Persons will not cross the bridges now except in large groups; small parties arriving at one end of a bridge wait till several arrive and all cross together. Shoes being very scarce and too expensive for almost anyone to buy, are articles sometimes "requisitioned" by the robbers, and from feet that are walking in snow, too! Some amusing tales are told of those who have luck, though robbed. I believe the following to be true: One gentleman had his handsome fur coat removed from his shoulders on a very cold night; he told one of the soldiers who had robbed him that he wished his old uniform coat, in order that he might not freeze. The soldier gave it to him and he wore it home, where he searched the pockets and found eight thousand rubles! Another gentleman, with even more quickness of wit, saved his warm coat by saying, "Why do you rob *me*; I just took this coat from a 'Bourgeoisie' not five minutes ago!" You see one has a laugh occasionally.

Some officers (in disguise) from Sevastopol have been here with the usual request. They tell us the officers were murdered there because they refused to fight against the Cossacks; that is to say, against General Kalédin, who has been trying to keep Bolshevism out of the Don Country; also, the lists of the officers who served on the mutiny courts-martial in 1905 and 1912 were found by the anarchists, and the officers were killed; some of them were old men long since retired, but they were murdered just the same.

There is an alienist in this apartment house, one of the best known doctors in Russia, who has charge of a large insane asylum in Petrograd. He tells us he must soon release all his patients because he has no means of providing food for them. I suggested that Smolny would be a good place to confine them. The Rumanian Minister and his staff have left, being escorted to Torneo by "prominent Bolsheviks." Troubles between the Rumanian Army and the Bolsheviks continue.

We received another large mail, but still none of our couriers may leave. We are very glad to get such good news of what our country is doing for the war, and particularly happy that all of our loved ones are well. A mail is a perfect God-send here!

I am hoping that Walter will receive orders to other duty. There is absolutely nothing that can be accomplished here now, and one healthy man, with a good record and education, is being wasted here when his own country is at war! He is philosophical about it, realizing that Washington *cannot* understand the conditions here, but I see that he longs to be doing something worthwhile. I can't tell you how glad I am that I am here. He will avoid unnecessary personal encounters with the "Reds" all around us, but also that if they finally overcome us they will not be able to say, "It was easy!"

Fortunately there are three kinds of thermometers in use here, Fahrenheit, Centigrade and Reaumur; to convert a reading from one to another requires so many mental gymnastics that the effort raises my temperature! My domestic duties are now a real cross; the cook is a Bolshevik; it is almost impossible to get anything done the way I wish it done. When you take me for an automobile ride, on my return, and run out of gasoline, I will tell you of some of my troubles here. If I conceal nothing you will forget you are stranded!

An interesting naval order has appeared in the newspapers. Every man in the Russian Navy is now a "seaman," and all wear the same uniform. Some are to be "elected" to command; they will be called "Seaman Chief," or "Seaman Assistant Chief"; others, properly elected, of course, are to be called "Citizen Chief of Bureau," "Citizen Naval Attaché," etc.! Again it would be amusing if it were not so serious.

There is a very great deal of illness here, owing to lack of food, medicines, and other necessities.

The new legal arrangements are unique. There are to be no lawyers; some judges are to be "elected" (really appointed by Smolny) and they also act as jury. The accused is brought into court and the audience is invited to argue his case; anyone may testify; a farce! Mr. Trotsky (or someone else) makes a statement, immediately followed by "It is therefore proved that (statement repeated)," and it is considered unhealthy to contradict any statement made by those having offices at Smolny.

Again I close with the hope I can soon send this, but without any knowledge on that subject. Good Night! Happy New Year!

Affectionately,

No. 8 French Quay,
Petrograd,
February 10, 1918.

My dear—

Once more I am obliged to use my formula and say there is nothing new under the Russian sun! I have been to see many of my Russian friends; all are in despair, and who can blame them! Many new and horrible decrees are promised by Smolny, and I suppose that many of them will eventually go into effect. The madmen now ruling Russia, be they in Berlin or Petrograd, seem to be determined she must be entirely ruined. The ex-Ministers, also Colonel Kalpashnikov, are still in Peter and Paul, and our last note from the Colonel says the health of all is failing. For some weeks nothing but "Kerensky money" (printed while he was "ruler") could be obtained from the banks and Petrograd is flooded with that money; we now learn it is to be declared of no value, which, if done, will further pauperize those who have been rich.

Evening entertainments are not fashionable! People prefer to stay at home. We do go out by day and by night, but I am always glad to get safely home again. One simply *can't* stay in the house all the time. I am still "doing my bit" on Thursdays, and it affords about the only real pleasure I have; my friends come early now, and very few ladies remain after dark. The "annoyances" have now extended beyond the Allies; the Danish Legation was entered for an alleged food search, but the mob left after a telephone protest by Minister Scavenius[23] had been made to Smolny, and without taking any of the food.

A new idea has come from the Baltic Fleet, where the "committees" declare the ships to be "autonomous." I am in doubt as to just what that means, and no one seems able to enlighten me, but most likely it is the Bolshevik for "pirates," or "piracy." The worst of it is that the end is not yet; if we could say: "But we will win the war anyway," and have that statement end it, all would not be so bad. *But*, the world *cannot* afford to leave Russia as she will be when the big war is won, and it will take years to repair the harm that has been done to the whole world by the lack of decisive action here. Russians have frankly said to me: "You know we never hated Germany as a nation, and since the Allies have not saved us, it is perfectly natural we should rejoice if Germany saves us from these horrible beasts now running our country!" A *Bolshevik officer* told one of Walter's "scouts" that the average number of murders in Petrograd for last month was three hundred per day. I think that is *too* large, but it shows the belief of one who is in a position to get the reports. I am now an expert; I can tell what will not happen if nothing is done; Petrograd has qualified me!

One of the Army Officers attached to our Embassy is leaving soon for France and I hope to send this out by him. Our colony grows smaller, and that is as it should be, for this is no place for Americans! There is nothing that they can accomplish.

---

[23] Harald Scavenius (1873–1939) was Danish ambassador to Russia until the end of 1918.

We send much love to you all and assure you we will be very glad to see you some day!

Affectionately,

French Quay 8,
Petrograd,
February 20, 1918.

My dear—

This has been no time for writing letters! All of our previous surcharged atmosphere has been a mere nothing as compared with the last ten days. To be sure, the betrayal of Russia into the hands of Germany has continued successfully, and really nothing very *new* has turned up, but all that has gone before has now begun to pyramid, probably as per plan, and the air is heavy.

The anarchists have again threatened the American Ambassador and his staff, but I cannot see that any of them are awed! The thing that is properly causing uneasiness now is the rapid advance of a German Army in this direction. Possibly it advances for the sole purpose of driving the Allied Representatives from Petrograd. Now it is too late to interfere with the success of the plans for destruction, whoever made them; destruction is an accomplished fact.

I report that the Bolsheviks have changed the Russian calendar to make it coincide with ours! That will be a comfort to foreigners living in Russia and to business men with associations here.

The number of Russian officers who wish to join our Navy has increased with the decrease of Russia. One who had command of a destroyer when the Germans captured Riga Gulf told us that after the "fight" (?) was over and he was in retreat, he overtook a Russian battleship underway, but going very slowly; he went near, but saw no one and his hail was not answered. He finally put his destroyer alongside the battleship and some of his officers went on board. The battleship was *entirely deserted* but one of her engines was running as were her dynamos! Battle flags were flying and the ship was normal in all respects except there was not a soul on board! He could only find one place where she had been hit by a German shell, and no damage had been done there. He sunk the ship with one of his own torpedoes to prevent the Germans from getting her. And *that* is the way the "brave Red Russian sailors" (!!!) won (??) the battle of Riga Gulf!

Four days ago Walter and I received orders to shovel snow in the streets. The order reads:—(Translation.)

Mr. Walter and Pauline Crosley are detailed for forced labor (to shovel snow) on 18/5 February. The first named from 9:00 to 12:00 noon; the second named from 12:00 to 3:00 p. m.

(Sig.) Delegate of the House Committee, "T. VIASMESKAYA."

Walter declined to consider the order and announced that neither of us would do the work concerned; threats were made which have not yet been carried out. I have just learned for the first time that Walter has had a loaded carbine near the front door for some time, and he announces that there will be a very pretty fight when they try to make us shovel snow!

I did give another dinner party, and it will probably be the last one. The effort is simply too great for all concerned. Yesterday we called at the Spanish Legation; the wife of the Charge d'Affairs told me they had potatoes and tea for luncheon, only, and that, so far as she knew, there was nothing in the house for dinner!

The Embassy is trying to get a train ready to take all of us out by way of Siberia. Apparently it will soon be time to leave! I may *bring* this out of Russia! At any rate it will leave by the first reliable means and hope you will receive it.

Always affectionately,

Yours,

Chapter IX
EXIT FROM FINLAND

Grand Hotel,
Stockholm, Sweden,
April 1, 1918.

My dear—

"We're here because we're *here*!" When I last wrote you I had no idea that we would leave Petrograd before I could write you another letter, but we *did*! I have kept up my diary, and from it I will try to condense into one letter our very remarkable experiences and wanderings that have required five weeks, and some parts of which seem more like a nightmare than anything else I can think of or remember.

The very night after I wrote you the last letter we were advised by the Ambassador that we would leave Petrograd soon, a German army having made a rapid advance toward the city, and then being only twenty-four hours away, at the rate of its last advance, so all that night we packed our trunks, getting but two hours' sleep. The next day Walter was busy helping to get a train ready for the proposed flight to Siberia, and I completed our packing, leaving many things in order to reduce our baggage. The following day, Friday, February 22nd (a holiday!) I spent in packing trunks of Mr. and Mrs. McA. Smith with all of their beautiful things that would pack in trunks. Walter spent the day in completing arrangements for the train, burning his files and codes, closing out business affairs and transporting trunks! By that time transportation was most difficult to get and one had to accompany anything so carried to insure its delivery. Some people who did not do that lost all they had entrusted to the "lamovoy" (sled).

On Saturday, with all our baggage at the Embassy, ready to go to the Siberian train, the Ambassador asked Walter if he was willing to go out via Sweden, in order that Minister Ira Nelson Morris[1] there might learn just what conditions in Petrograd were. Upon being assured that he was willing, the Ambassador ordered him to go that way, and to leave Petrograd that night! There was another "hustle" to get baggage from the Embassy to the Finland Station, and to get there ourselves, we had planned to leave the next morning from the Nikolaevsky Station.[2] The matter of

---

[1] Ira Nelson Morris (1875–1942) was the American minister to Sweden, 1914–23.

[2] The railroad station from which one traveled to Moscow and on to Siberia.

passports was a serious one, but Walter, with the assistance of one of his able "scouts," who had served in the Foreign Office several years, managed to get in two hours, in the way of visas and permits, what others had not been able to get in two weeks. (It was expensive!)

Our train was due to leave at seven in the evening and we were there to take it, but it actually left near midnight of a cold, dark and depressing day. Some of *our* gloom was due to the valuable provisions we were obliged to leave behind; we gave away quantities of them, but had saved many cases to take on the Siberian train, where we had proposed to have a "community mess," each of us contributing what we had for a common store. There was no time to do anything with them and they were left in the apartment!

Several people, including the Ambassador, braved the storm and were at the station to say goodbye to us. We could get no accommodations on the train, and were fortunate indeed to find that the French Embassy had a day coach on the train which was not full, and we were permitted to travel in that. (It was filled many times during the night by joy-riding soldiers!) We had to sit up all night and it was so cold! What a miserable night it was!!

We were obliged to change cars at Rikimaki, for Helsingfors, where it was necessary for us to go in order to procure a Swedish visa and permission to travel on a Swedish steamer. We arrived at Helsingfors that afternoon, quite exhausted, and found that a room had been reserved for us at the Hotel Societets Husets, in accordance with a telegram Walter had sent to our Consul there. We counted the number of times we were required to show our passports between Petrograd and Helsingfors—*nineteen times*—but probably none of the Red Guard who looked at them could read! At the hotel we found two American couples who had left Petrograd ahead of us, and who were bound home, so we became a party of six, and decided to travel together. It required four days to complete the necessary formalities at Helsingfors, during which time Walter studied maps and learned all possible of the civil war then going on between the Red Guard of Finland (reinforced by Russian Bolsheviks and mercenary Russian soldiers) and the White Guard, composed of much the best element in Finland. They were commonly called the "Reds" and the "Whites."

The government of Sweden had sent some ice breakers from Stockholm to Mantyluoto, on the west coast of Finland, to rescue Swedish subjects, and we obtained permission to go to Stockholm in one of those, but could not learn when the next one would sail. We decided to go to Bjorneberg, near Mantyluoto, where we were more likely to get accommodations, and wait for the ice breaker, and where Walter had decided to be the best place to try to go through the firing lines of the "Reds" and the "Whites" if we were unable to get a steamer. In the meantime we had thoroughly enjoyed the relative quiet and cleanliness of Helsingfors, though there was a nine o'clock curfew rule, and frequent shooting on the streets at night. We found very much more food in Helsingfors than in Petrograd, and we even were able to buy some small apples, at thirty cents each! We also bought other provisions to carry with us, as we learned it was very difficult to get enough to eat further north. *How* we did sigh for the delicious provisions we had left behind! We had beautiful weather while in Helsingfors, and while forced to wait there, we walked and drove about the very pretty little city.

On February 28th we saw a *black flag, with skull and crossed bones* flying over what was once the Naval Officers Club, and where Walter had been entertained, but which had been taken and used as an anarchist club! I never expected to see that flag in actual use, but I have! The day before we left Helsingfors our friends of the Siberian Railway journey, Mr. and Mrs. Corse and Miss Potter, arrived from Petrograd, and there were nine of us. On March first we went by train to Bjoneborg where we found many refugees, and also a grave doubt about another ice breaker making the trip to Stockholm, as one had just been sunk in the ice! We also found little friendliness towards refugees in general at Bjoneborg, the natives rightly believing that we would eat considerable of their small food supply, and apparently not realizing that we did not particularly relish *being* refugees, nor was it our fault that we were. Bjoneborg is a small town, but neat and clean, with handsome wide streets excellently laid out.

There were many evidences of nearby fighting, including the wounded that were being brought in, and sometimes we could hear the firing; again we were in an armed camp! The refugees, representing many nations, held a mass meeting to discuss ways and means; the meeting was addressed by the ex-Chief of Police of the town, who advised us all to go back south, to Abo, and try to cross on the ice to the Aland Islands, thence to Stockholm by steamer. Walter knew there were German troops and ships between Abo and Stockholm and he advised the Americans not to go that way, assuring them that he would not try it. Many of the other refugees did try it; some were captured and a few got out that way.

Walter had been making the acquaintance of the Red leaders and presenting them with cigarettes and other things, thereby making a certain amount of friendship. This he continued during our entire forced stay in Finland, and the results showed that it was worthwhile. An attractive Finnish gentleman who spoke excellent English had volunteered to act as interpreter, there being no American with us who could speak Finnish. This gentleman placed us under great obligations by his kindness, as did also the Danish Consul and his efficient Secretary, who even arranged it so we could have *milk* delivered to us!

The refugees held another meeting and sent a rather curt note to the Red Guard Headquarters *demanding* that we be allowed to pass through the fighting lines. Walter refused to have anything to do with the protest and was not surprised when the Reds sent a written reply to the protest, assuring those who had made it that they could *not* go through! Later results showed that Walter's method of treating them produced more friendship. Walter had been able to send cables to the American Legation here (Stockholm), notifying them of our predicament, and requesting their assistance in getting an ice breaker for the Americans, the number having grown in the meantime by the assembling of those who had gotten out of Petrograd earlier and later. The final reply from the Legation indicated that we could not hope for a steamer.

In the meantime he continued "cultivating" the Red Guard, but on March fifth we were all ordered to leave Bjoneborg at once! The Reds were evidently tired of being bothered by refugees. At the same time we received a telegram from our Consul at Helsingfors informing us he had made arrangements for an "American train" to go through the lines north of Tammerfors, and advising us to join the train at that place. It seemed too good to be true, but we made another grand scramble to catch the daily train, and went to Tammerfors, where we soon learned that the "American train" was only a partial verbal promise! There were two "trains" there at that time; one contained the British Embassy from Petrograd and the other the remaining Embassies and Legations representing the Allies in Petrograd, which had not left via Siberia. The occupants of the British train got through the fighting lines as per plan, but the Reds claimed that the Whites took military advantage of the armistice, and refused to allow any other foreigners to leave Tammerfors! They also developed a very annoying suspicion that all of us were spies, which was dangerous for us!

We were prisoners, but we had plenty of company, there being nearly three hundred people aboard the "Allied Train," among them some of our best friends in the Diplomatic Corps of Petrograd. The French Ambassador was the "Doyen" of the "Train," and he invited us to attach our American car thereto, but fortunately Walter decided against it, for, after a very tiresome and "heart-breaking" delay at Tammerfors, with many acrimonious conferences, the Allied Train was ordered to leave for the *South*, and did so, while the Americans kept very inconspicuous in their various lodgings. While representatives from the Allied Train were apparently creating an unfavorable impression among the Red leaders, Walter was trying to make friends with them, had received certain concessions, and had employed a most competent young woman as interpreter.

By the way, the first night we arrived at Tammerfors no accommodations could be found for some hours and we had painful visions of sitting up all night in the cold and dreary railroad station. With the assistance of this interpreter we finally slept in a hospital that night. The next day we found a room in a *very* inferior hotel! Food was getting more and more scarce, and we did not dare to eat the small amount we were carrying because we might find ourselves absolutely without provisions, at any time. Other Americans joined us at Tammerfors and still more assembled at Helsingfors; these passed through Tammerfors, en route for Bjoneborg, while we remained there to deal with the Reds.

We were living on the top floor, up three long flights of stairs and imagine our gratitude to the dear Portuguese Minister, Mr. Batalha-Reis,[3] who was quite an elderly gentleman, when he climbed all those steps and notified Walter confidentially that the Allied Train would leave immediately, inviting us to share his car! Walter assured him of his great appreciation, but told him he could not desert the other Americans, and the train left for Toyola. We were more lonesome but the absence of the diplomats gave Walter a better chance to continue making friends with the Red leaders, of which he took advantage, and finally obtained permission for *all Americans* to assemble at Bjoneborg, which was *North*, not *South*, of Tammerfors!

We made our plans to leave, and were actually on the train, "bag and baggage," when some Red Guards came in our car with bayonets on their rifles and ordered us to get out! The train was held one hour while Walter, assisted by the British Consul, argued the matter, but the Chief, who had given the necessary permission, was out of town, his subordinates did not understand the situation, and we had to leave the train! It began to look as though we were doomed to spend the summer in Finland!

Walter again "cultivated" (expensively) the Reds and once more obtained permission to go to Bjoneborg; this time we were allowed to proceed and we joined the other Americans at that place. In the meantime Professor and Mrs. Emory [?]had left our party and tried to reach Stockholm via Abo and the Aland Islands; they were captured by the Germans, Mrs. Emory being allowed to go on and her husband being taken to Germany a prisoner. We found her here when we arrived.

There followed a very tiresome and tiring week at Bjoneborg, during which time Walter renewed his friendships with the Reds and decided that the Legation at Stockholm and the Consulate at Helsingfors could not get us out of Finland; he proposed to the other Americans that he be permitted to make the effort entirely alone, the others to do and say nothing except what he requested. They all agreed, and he immediately employed all of them, in order that he might truthfully say that all were employees of the United States Government, and that he was their leader. Now the friends he had made among the Reds began to be of real service, and on Sunday, March 24th, we *got out*; the best way to tell you about that is to copy my diary, written at the time, so here it is for that day:

Sunday, March 24, 1918. At Bjoneborg and crossing the lines. Began fine day, but partly cloudy; very cold and windy *on ice*. Up at 6:45 a. m. to get away for Mantyluoto. Left Bjoneborg at 9:15 in special sleeping car with baggage car attached, seventeen of us as follows: Captain and Mrs. W. S. Crosley, Lieutenant and Mrs. N. C. Stines, Mr. and Mrs. F. M. Corse, Miss Potter, Mr. A. F. Bull, Mr. E. G. Sisson, Mr. G. C. Smith, Mr. R. E. Simmons, Mr. J. J. Tyer, Mr. T. O. Larsen, Mr. A. Guranesco (Rumanian),

---

[3] Jaime Batalha-Reis (1847–1934) was the Portuguese minister to Russia and the delegate from Portugal to the Versailles Peace Conference in 1919.

Mr. and Mrs. Sgwodoveski and child (Poles, Naturalized Americans), Miss Ranta, Interpreter.

Arrived Mantyluoto 9:50 a. m., W. S. C. (in uniform), Mr. Tyer and Miss Ranta left for Red firing lines in sleigh, under escort of Red Guards. Drove until 11:00 a.m., meeting Red Chief Eloranta[4] at his Headquarters en route, on an island in Gulf of Bothnia. He went to front with them. They carried a large silk American flag, property of Mrs. Corse, and one belonging to Mrs. McA. Smith, also a white flag. Planted them on parapet of natural stone fort in most advanced position. There was considerable firing from White Front. Could hear bullets and see them hit ice. Red Chief sent out couriers to order his men to cease firing, which they did. Whites fired for nearly an hour, then quit. W. S. C. went on ice with American flag, followed by Mr. Tyer with white flag. Miss Ranta followed Mr. Tyer. No shots, but they soon found they could not walk on the ice. Wind was too strong and ice too slippery. Eloranta brought out horse and bobsled behind them. All three got on board and W. S. C. drove over to White Lines, where they were received by *gentlemen* but were arrested. Walked and drove about ten versts to the Headquarters of the District, and were met by Lieutenant C. F. Diehl, of the Swedish Army, who is a volunteer serving with the Whites, and Chief of Staff to Captain Palvela, in command of District. Had interview, coffee, bread *and butter*, for two hours, then, having made all arrangements for passage of entire party, also baggage, W. S. C. started back to Mantyluoto, by way of the Island, in same bob-sled with their horse, which Whites tried to keep, but gave up on protest of W. S. C. who had purchased it from the Reds. It was with difficulty and after much argument W. S. C. and Tyer were permitted to return, and Miss Ranta, being a Finn, was detained in accordance with their orders not to permit *anyone* to return to Red side. They reached train at Mantyluoto at 3:45 p. m., started our party and baggage for Red front in sleighs, eleven sleighs and sledges in all, W. S. C. and Lieut. Stines being in last one.

Reds took us to point midway between lines and left us and our baggage on the ice. (*Very cold.*) Teams returned to Red Lines and more teams from White Lines came out to pick us up. Miss Ranta, in accordance with instructions from W. S. C. arranged in meantime for Reds to be allowed to go on the ice and remove some of their dead. This they did, Eloranta walking out alone, with sleigh following him, while White teams were taking our baggage ashore, W. S. C. and Tyer having driven back to Red Lines and told them they could remove their dead. Red Chief (Eloranta) headed *our* calvacade to middle point, carrying our largest American flag. He was a brave man, for he believed the Whites would shoot him in spite of our presence! Eloranta was very happy because of the permission to remove his dead. Reds had

---

[4] Frans Evert Eloranta (1879–1936) was a Finnish socialist who served in the Finnish Parliament and later as the commander in chief of the Finnish Red Guard.

considerable sentiment concerning the dead and did not want to leave them on the ice. Their sentiment prompted great gratitude to us.

Whole party was taken in sleighs and sledges to village of Ahlaiten, White District Headquarters. Twelve (12) hours from time we left Bjoneborg we were in White lines. That night we were considerably divided for sleeping quarters. After a *hot supper* and plenty to eat, also much milk to drink, we separated to: private houses, schools, barracks, churches and barns, where we slept in much *mental* comfort. The physical comfort was not so considerable, but we were glad to be there. We were treated *most* kindly and considerately by the Commander of the District and his subordinates, and we were as grateful as one can be. Mr. Guranesco, Rumanian First Secretary of Legation, was particularly glad to have his struggles of travel of more than three months from Jassy practically finished in safety.

We slept very well in spite of strange surroundings and the small reddish-brown insects that seemed too plentiful! We got to bed at 2:00 a.m. There! That is the history of one strenuous day!

The next day we started in eleven sleighs and sleds, up the Gulf of Bothnia, for Christinestadt, where we arrived at eleven P. M., after a perfectly wonderful ride, which was *very cold!* We changed horses once, and how those tough Finnish ponies did fly over the ice!! It interested me very much to see ours grab a mouthful of snow while trotting very fast; it was his way of getting a drink! I shall never forget the beautiful sunset over the frozen Gulf of Bothnia, and the wonderful moonlight reflected from the snow until one could almost read the print of a newspaper; but it was *cold*! We were in the last sleigh, and the winding calvacade ahead of us in those lights was impressive. We scattered for the night in Christinestadt, sleeping where we could find places, and the next day took a train for Sinioki, the Headquarters of General Mannerheim, Chief of the White Guards.

Our Minister at Stockholm had sent the Assistant Military Attaché of the Legation to Sinioki to assist us, and the wonderful hot supper he had prepared for us on our arrival, as well as the sleeping quarters for which we did not have to search, made us most grateful to him, and we felt that at last we were out of trouble. That was not quite the case! We left Sinioki early the next morning and arrived at Torneo, on the boundary between Finland and Sweden, at midnight, too late to cross the frontier that night, and there was no place in the town for us to sleep! We were permitted to stay in our very uncomfortable car, which was backed out into the woods, and we slept as best we could, sitting up in our clothes, *but*, the fire in the stove went out and again it was *so* cold!

The following morning our car was taken back to Torneo, and a long and tiresome morning with the passport control officers and customs officials ensued. At noon we crossed in sleighs to Haparanda, Sweden, during a roaring blizzard, but how thankful we all were when we saw the Swedish flag flying and realized that we were really *out of Russia*! We spent the afternoon in a good hotel, in the meantime managing to charter a luxurious sleeping car for our sole use, and at eight o'clock that night we left for Stockholm, a very happy party of refugees and refugettes!

I mentioned the scarcity of food in Finland,—and I must place on record one case of the high cost of living there; I will probably always remember that in one place we paid seventy-two cents *each* for eggs; possibly we paid more in proportion for something else, I am not sure, but that price I have remembered with a resentful feeling! We slept better in our special car than we had for some time, and enjoyed a beautiful day of travel through an interesting country after we woke up; we actually had a dining car on the train. Such luxury! That night was one of comfort, also, and we arrived here at noon, two days ago, very much pleased with ourselves! We were met at the station by Minister Ira Nelson Morris and his secretaries, with his automobile to take us to the hotels where our reservations had been made by the Legation, and this kind attention on his part was very greatly appreciated by our entire party. We came to this hotel, and now we are in the greatest comfort we have had for many months, and we are not hungry!

Walter has received orders to go to Madrid, Spain, which distresses him very much because he cannot get into real military service, but which he feels he cannot ask to have changed. Therefore we leave here for Madrid as soon as we can get passage across the North Sea, and you will next hear from me in London. It has been a very interesting, exciting and tiresome thirteen months since we left New York, but I would not have missed it for worlds, tho' I *am* thankful for the coming prospect of life without Bolshevism.

Before I end this I must put in one plea about that most horrible disease! *Please*, as you are a patriot, use every means within your power to prevent that disease from getting a start in the United States. There is no step too difficult to be well warranted, for the only cure for Bolshevism is death to it! With much love for all from both of us.

Affectionately yours,
PAULINE.

AFTERWORD

Since I have returned to the United States, my friends have asked me a great many "whys?" about Russia. The one most often heard is "Why did Russia quit?" The simplest answer to this is "Because Germany wanted her to quit," but this answer involves many ramifications.

First. All Russia was tired of the three years of war and Russian people, as a whole, lack that patriotism which inspired the individuals of the British armies and the French armies to fight on in the face of adversity. Being weary, it was easy for efficient German propaganda to make traitors of Russian soldiers.

Second. The Russian governing machine was corrupt. This is too well known by all students of Russian history to need proof. Its corruption made it easy for Germans to introduce their representatives into the machine. Once there they could not only influence the delivery of munitions but also the very military policies, to German advantage.

Third. A great many of the best Russian officers and soldiers were killed during the years of the war that preceded the Revolution. What was left did not represent the best that was in Russians (speaking generally).

Fourth. The real ignorance of the great majority of Russians made their brains ready receptacles for the false information poured into them by paid German agents, highly organized and efficient, as well as by fanatical anarchists who cared nothing for anyone or anything but their own pet theories. There was no efficient Ally organization to combat the German efforts, and Russians do not possess executive ability enough to organize against them.

Fifth. Probably *no one* in Washington, London, Paris or Rome anticipated what would happen in Russia. Very few in Petrograd, or elsewhere, in Russia, anticipated it. Least of all did the educated Russians anticipate it. For these reasons the efforts of the few who could and did look ahead to organize against what seemed inevitable to them were futile. I know that all Allied representatives lacked the essential money to combat the German machine. When a small amount of money became available, it was too late, and the amounts were too small to have been of real value at any time.

Sixth. Russian officers, educated and patriotic men, lacked those qualities of organization and leadership which could at any time, (and could even now), have interposed efficient military force against the armed rabble at first representing the power of the Bolsheviks.

Seventh—and greatest! The Russian character is a peculiar one, and but little understood by any foreigners. The Germans understand it best. Russians themselves do not understand Russians. Many of my good Russian friends have said: "You foreigners amuse us. You visit Russia for a few months and write a book about Russia, believing you understand Russians, when we, who are Russians, and have always lived here, do not understand ourselves! We do not know what we will do next!"

Many true anecdotes will illustrate the foregoing: A titled Russian of great education and experience, who, with his charming and cultivated Russian wife frequently visited our home, was in the habit of complaining that the Allies had deserted Russia. These two were as patriotic and able as any Russians I know, and they suffered mental agony because of the ruination of Russia. Finally the following was proposed to this gentleman: "Assume that you have been in New York for a year; that your wife joins you there having come direct from Petrograd, that she relates to you what is now happening in Petrograd and in Russia. Would you believe it?" After a few minutes of thought he replied, "No—I *could* not!" He was then asked, "How can you expect an American in Washington, who has never seen Russia, to believe it?" After more thought he replied, "You are right, they *can't* believe it!"

One method of the Bolsheviks will illustrate how they obtained the services of the officers. The "Committee" of a certain destroyer decided they would enjoy going in their vessel to Petrograd, announcing that they were not pleased by the methods of the "government" and would bombard the city. The following conversation took place between the "Committee" and the officer "in command"(?)

Committee: "You will navigate the ship to Petrograd in order that we may bombard."

Officer: "I certainly will not!"

Committee: "Very well, we will kill you and get someone else!"

Officer: "I am ready to be killed but am not ready to cause the death of many innocent unfortunates in the Capital!"

Committee: "Oh—in that case we will not kill you, but will go ashore and kill your wife and children!"

It can readily be seen why the officer yielded and took the vessel to Petrograd.

The Red Guard would "arrest" an officer. He would be told he must fight in their ranks. He would decline, but when assured what would otherwise happen to his family he would agree. Many officers were asked why their fellows who had been murdered did not resist. The invariable reply was, "It would madden the beasts and they would kill *all* of the 'intelligentsia'"! Whether or not this is true, they believed it. Officers were acting as porters at the railroad stations and as laborers; were selling newspapers on the streets; were peddling what they could find to sell from house to house. Their wives were pawning jewelry and other valuables. They must do something or starve, and they *were* starving. Frequently they would be prevented from working in order to increase their misery. Under these actual conditions it is not difficult to understand why they did not stop the destruction of Russia.

A group of officers once visited my husband and offered eighteen hundred officers for him to command and capture Petrograd. They did not understand his amazement that among that many officers there were no leaders! They did not understand why he could not accept their proposition!

Shortly after his arrival in Russia, my husband decided that serious efforts were necessary to keep Russia in the war; he developed a plan which required money for its use; an elderly wealthy Russian Countess, with a wonderful education and who knew nearly everyone of her class in Russia, appealed to him for advice as to how the Russian intelligent class could help retain Russians on the firing lines. He replied that he needed three reliable Russian gentlemen, one civilian, one army officer and a naval officer, *who could be trusted*. He asked the Countess if she knew three such men. She replied, "But of course! I could trust them with my jewels, my money, my honor, everything!" He said: "I need three men to whom we can tell a great secret in confidence, and be *sure* that all Petrograd will not know about it within a week!" The Countess thought seriously for a time and said, sadly, "I am afraid I do not know any such Russians!" This illustrates a phase of Russian character. Past masters of intrigue, their plots, counter-plots, and counter-counter-plots throve, each one to be thwarted because of "leaks"!

The educated Russian is a wonderful friend, and one of the most attractive people of the earth. The Russian peasant is also a lovable character, until crazed by vodka or mental poison. His great strength makes him dangerous then. Russians, as a whole, have been likened unto grown children. This is true in great part, but differs in that a child becomes mentally and physically tired sooner than a Russian. Several Russians have told me that a Russian giant of a peasant will weep bitterly after he murders his first victim, but he glories in the act after his second and third!

Representatives of every walk in Russian life have told me they wished the Czar were back in power, but probably as many similar representatives expressed their hope that the Germans would soon arrive to produce law and order! They were weary of strife and effort but it is probably true that they tire sooner than some other nations. There is no doubt in my mind but that the ultimate salvation of Russia depends upon education, this term being used in its broadest sense, and most certainly including a knowledge of other peoples. Real discipline is rare in Russia. The Cossacks have rigid discipline in their homes, therefore, it follows them even to death in the ranks. Others have, in general, only the discipline inspired by fear of one sort or another, and the revulsion of feeling when that fear is removed, can readily be understood.

I am not at all sure it is the duty of the United States to bring order out of chaos in Russia, as she has done elsewhere in certain islands, but I *am* sure it is the duty of someone, with the ultimate end in view of their self-government *when they are ready for it*. No relatively ignorant people can govern themselves while in contact with an advanced outside world. Russians have been (easily) deceived into believing they can govern themselves now. As the methods adopted are those of anarchy, no discussion of them is necessary. Only fanatics believe anarchy to be good. To *feed* Lenin and Trotsky is to nourish anarchy. There is but one answer to that. Don't!

Before going to Russia (or to Armenia) it *might* be well for American troops to suppress some of the lawlessness in the United States.

If I have been suspected of leaning toward monarchy, be it known that I am for law and order, also, for whatever form of representative government will bring them about. Under the Bolsheviks there has not been law and order in Russia. Their "government" cannot be called *representative* by even the most fanatical.

If it is thought I use the word "officers" too often, it should be understood that all Russian gentlemen did military service, and, a great war being on, practically all of my men-friends were naturally officers.

APPENDIX
Samples of Enemy Propaganda

City—Petrograd.
Paper—*Commune* of September, 1917.
Subject—War Loans.

DOWN WITH WAR LOANS

Which is the great question of the holy war in the name of great ideas? Listen and you shall hear:

The loan of five billion dollars! Unlimited credit to the allies.

Why is it required in the holy war that the first step be the transfer of money not of men? Five billion dollars have been issued by the Government of the United States of America to the allied Powers. Why? What has happened before, which could involve such a step? It means simply that the American money-kings are sending the American people to get back their money which has been involved in the European war, and also with large interest.

The war loan has become too large. Morgan[1] and the other members of the Stock Exchange have financed the European war, but they went too far and could not stop. Their side did not win quickly enough and the loans grew to hundreds of millions, until the balance itself was found in danger. To refuse the Allies the money was also impossible, because in that case the Allies could not finish the war and would therefore be unable to repay any money. Day by day the loan grew larger and larger and troubled the heart of the Exchange.

It is true that at the end the Allies would have won, but the nervous strain of waiting was too depressing for the Exchange gamblers, who usually have a habit of making sure of their success.

Their ideas to refuse to pay out the war loans gladdened the hearts of the European armies.

Therefore it was obligatory to involve the American government and oblige it to save the situation. An army had to be organized as well as a navy, and the public opinion was that they came into the war to save their money. In reality

---

[1] J. P. Morgan (1867–1943) was the prominent American banker who loaned several countries money during World War I.

this was a war for the honor...of our banks. The result of a defeat meant the ruin of the United States, otherwise of the parasites of the United States.

All offenses from France and England were forgotten and ignored, because France and England were too dangerous to be touched.

The Government of the United States, in fact, guaranteed to buy up the bills of Morgan & Company, and two millions of American soldiers will be sent as soon as possible to France, to kill the Germans.

No, not the Germans, but to kill French syndicalists, when they, at the end of the war will throw in the face of Morgan his bills with the words:—"To hell with the dollars. I will repay you when you give me back the lives of our brothers."

You, stupid German patriots, do not be afraid. The American navy and army will not touch the Kaiser. They will go to Europe to kill the French and to renew the "order" and the war loans at the end of war, and to quell the rising French revolution.

Do not think that Russia is the only country which has attained a revolution in this war.

Let us suppose that after the end of the war the people of England, France, Russia, Italy, Germany and Austria will come to some conclusion that the war loans are too large and cannot be repaid. The very thought of such a possibility has made the Exchange shake with terror, and immediately the New York banks have issued an order "to send representatives of the United States to the Peace Conference, because the payment of the war loans must not be refused."

Do not believe the words of the revolutionary press. Here are the words of E. P. Harding from the "Federal Reserve Board" dated March 22nd, 1917, as follows: "As a banker and a creditor, the United States must have a place at the table of the Peace Conference and therefore have a possibility to have a word should the question of the repayment of war loans be raised. We must remember that we will have to use a stick to force the debtors of our citizens to pay their debts."

In other words—an army which will score in its ranks from two to five million men, is an army which America has to have on the field of France for the time when the diplomats will gather round the table to solve the question of the repayment of the war loans.

Do not let yourself be duped! Financial reasons were at the back of every movement from the outbreak of the war, and here also we are up against a business proposition—the declaration of war by the American Exchange.

I trust that all the countries will follow the steps of Russia. It is a fact that a million French soldiers in the trenches are already saying that war loans ought to be abolished and their children released from everlasting servitude.

APPENDIX

The abolishment of war loans will be even more than the Russian revolution. It would mean a complete destruction of tyranny and poverty, and would once for all kill imperialism and maybe even capitalism.

This is the weakest part of our money-kings, and this is where we have to strike. It is the only vulnerable place, and you have to deliver your death-blow to the gigantic universal money autocracy.

Proper propaganda in America, Russia, France, Germany and England is indispensable.

sig. B. Miner.

POLITICAL NOTE
October 12–25, 1917.
Translated by Prince.

THE NORTHERN DISTRICT CONFERENCE OF COUNCILS OF WORKMEN' S AND SOLDIERS' DELEGATES.
(Ryetch 12–25. October, 1917)

The conference opened on the 11th–24th of October. Present 103 delegates including a representative from the Moscow Soviet.

The recently released Bolshevik prisoner, sublieutenant Krilenko (comrade Abram) was elected chairman.

A number of very outspoken speeches were made at this meeting and the speakers spoke very definitely about their proposed actions and intentions.

A representative from the Finnish Councils offered to send a delegation to the "Kresty" prison to transmit the greetings of the conference to the

Bolsheviks who were imprisoned there. This motion was accepted.

The chairman of the Petrograd Soviet, Trotsky, made a report on the work his organization was doing. He announced that the Petrograd Council is at present a "strong" body and is conducting a relentless war against the classes and is standing on an irreconcilable position against all supporting the provisional Government. He also said that it is evident that it has been decided to surrender Petrograd to the enemy, but the Soviet will not leave Petrograd. The Staff has decided to take the garrison from the city, but the Petrograd Council has not decided to give its stamp of approval to this order, as it has no guarantees that this order has been made only for strategic purposes. Tomorrow or the day after the Petrograd garrison will have to face the question as to whether it is willing to submit to this order of the Staff or not.

In conclusion Trotsky spoke of the necessity to hand over the government and management of the country into the hands of the Soviets, attacked the Government, etc.

The representative of the Baltic Fleet announced that the fleet does not recognize the Provisional Government; that the latter has been informed that it should not clog the telegraph with its orders, as the latter will all the same not be executed.

Regarding the last sea battles this representative said the following: When it became known that the German fleet is seeking to engage the Russian in battle, then the commander of the Baltic Fleet came to the second conference of the Baltic fleet organizations and asked if the sailors would execute the battle orders of the Commanding Personnel. The conference informed him that the battle orders under the control of the conference Commissaire would be executed, but that the orders of the Government would not be obeyed, whereby the Commander of the Fleet was warned, that if he did not execute any order of the Commissaire of the council, he would be the first to hang on the first mast available.

He also stated that the Baltic fleet was the victor in the uneven battle with the German fleet, as it had suffered less loss than its adversary. What will happen further is not known. The fleet is suffering for want of articles of primal necessity. It is possible that the sailors of the Baltic fleet will be the first to enter into an armistice to save the fleet. In conclusion the speaker in the name of the Baltic Fleet cursed Kerensky and announced that the fleet stands for a further deepening of the revolution.

Trotsky after this speech offered to welcome the men of the Baltic fleet which was accepted unanimously.

The Moscow delegate announced that the Moscow region is on the eve of closing the works and factories owing to the shortage of fuel and raw materials.

The representative of the Finland District Committee announced that the Committee is closely watching the activity of the Government in Finland. Finland, he said, is on the eve of civil war, the Finnish bourgeoisie is armed and is ready to give battle to the proletariat. The duty of the Committee is to disarm the bourgeoisie and hand the arms over to the proletariat.

Great interest was attracted to the speech of the representative of the Petrograd district councils of Soviets, who said that in that body the representative of the Louga Soviet announced that it would send 30,000 bayonets to Petrograd to subdue the Bolsheviks in case of trouble.

This announcement caused tremendous indignation in the council, which is largely Bolshevik. The Petrograd district conference has decided, according to the speaker, to take the authority into its hands, following the example of Kronstadt.

The representative of the Helsingfors Soviet said that in his town the whole authority is already in the hands of the Soviet.

The Kronstadt representative was warmly received and stated that the Kronstadt Council followed the correct system from the beginning, by taking all authority into its hands. The speaker considers that it is necessary to assemble with the all-Russian council of Soviets, which alone can convene a revolutionary Constituent Assembly.

The Wiborg delegate stated that there the council took the place, after their drowning, of the Commandant and Corps Commander, and that at present all the authority in the town is in the hands of the Council.

The Representative of Reval expressed himself against the evacuation of that town, as it is considered that this measure will weaken the Proletariat of the town. The tendency in Reval is Bolshevik, but during the last days the revolutionary wave is beginning to diminish. Therefore the Reval Soviet refuses to take the authority into its hands.

Representatives from the front also spoke. A Corps Representative said that in his Corps a general had been killed and 60 officers arrested as suspected counter revolutionists.

Representatives of a fusilier regiment said that the regiment had decided that an armistice should be arranged not later than the 1st of November on all the fronts. After that date the regiments will act independently.

The representative of the Volyn regiment said that it would not leave Petrograd, without taking the Provisional Government with it.

The chairman in summarizing the opinions of the conference came to the conclusion that the majority of the Councils represented are opposed to the Provisional Government. The Majority of the Councils demand the handing over of the government to the Councils.

THE PRESENT RUSSIAN SITUATION

(Newspaper article in *November*, 1917, published before the Bolsheviks were well seated in the saddle.)

Now that all hopes for victory of law-abiding democracy over radical socialism represented by the Bolsheviks, who do not recognize any law or precedent, except such as they have made themselves, have been shattered by the failure of the Constituent Assembly to gather round itself sufficient forces to exist, protect its members and execute their orders, it is no use to build any hopes for the future on the chances of the rapid downfall of Bolshevism or its defeat by another faction of Socialism in Russia. That Russia is socialistic to the roots is now established beyond any doubts, as of the 500-odd members of the Constituent Assembly only 15 belong to non-Socialist parties, namely the Constitutional Democrats (Kadets). The only two political groups now that can be considered of any importance in shaping the future of the country are the Socialist Revolutionaries and the Social Democrats, Maximalists or the Bolsheviks.

The Socialist Revolutionaries are now in a state of confusion and disintegration; a large part of the party has already joined the Bolshevik wing, this is the Left Socialist Revolutionary faction led by Spiridonova,[2] Steinberg,[3] etc.; the remaining ones are grouping themselves now round Tchernov[4] who was elected chairman of the Constituent Assembly; the former strong Breshko-Breshkovski,[5] Kerensky and Avksientiev[6] group is no longer visible politically. The main fault of the Social Revolution has been their lack of firmness and cooperation, each leader trying to overcome his party comrades, rather than to combat the outside enemies.

---

[2] Maria Spiridonova (1885–1941) was a member of the Party of Socialists-Revolutionaries, and at the age of twenty-one attempted to assassinate a government official in Tambov for the brutal repression of a peasant uprising. Spiridonova was raped, beaten, and tortured, and sent to Siberia. She was released in March 1917, and soon became leader of the Party of the Left Socialist Revolutionaries and worked with the Bolsheviks until 1918, after which she began to actively oppose them. During subsequent years she was repeatedly arrested and eventually exiled to Central Asia and Siberia, and in 1941, she was shot to prevent her capture by advancing German troops.

[3] Isaac Nachman Steinberg (1888–1957) was a member of the Socialist Revolutionary Party who received the position of minister of justice in Lenin's first government. He later resigned his position in protest of the signing of the treaty with Germany in March 1918, the Treaty of Brest-Litovsk. During the 1930s and early 1940s, he lived abroad, and was an active leader in the movement to find safe havens for Jewish refugees.

[4] Victor Chernov (1873–1952) was a co-founder of the pro-peasant Party of Socialists-Revolutionaries, one of the largest revolutionary parties before the revolution. He served briefly in the Provisional Government as minister of agriculture in 1917. He left Russia after the Russian Civil War (1918–21) and remained abroad until his death.

[5] Ekaterina Breshko-Breshkovskaya (1844–1934) was one of the oldest of the political activists, and as such became known to the others as "Babushka," which means "grandmother." During 1917, she supported Kerensky and the Provisional Government, and after the revolution, she joined the forces fighting against the Bolsheviks.

[6] Nikolai Avksentiev (1878–1943) was an active member of the Socialist Revolutionary Party and a notable orator, but in the immediate years before World War I, he disavowed terror. In 1917, he supported Kerensky and served as minister of the interior in the Provisional Government. He opposed the Bolshevik seizure of power and participated in anti-Bolshevik activities after the revolution. He died in New York City.

APPENDIX 145

The Social Democrats, Minimalists, or the Menshiviki, although including such brilliant men as Skobelev[7] and Tzeretelli[8] are very weak in numbers.

The Bolsheviks after their success in October are moving forward along definite and clearly outlined lines; they do not hide their purposes as the methods they are now employing and planning indicate. Their program, which they demanded that the Constituent Assembly accept or be dismissed, is complete and clear. They do not hide the fact that they do not believe in a Government of all the people, they say that their aims can be only achieved by a class government, the government of the laboring and the exploited. They demand that all the other classes should be abolished and destroyed and state that they will do this by a general labor system, that is, nobody will have a free choice in determining his occupation, but will do what he is ordered to do by the Government, or really by the local self-government of the workmen and poor peasants. Inasmuch as all the banks are closed and have been so for weeks all state loans are canceled and companies are forbidden to pay dividends on stocks; all the population of Russia has to live on is what it earns or die of hunger. So far a certain modus vivendi is still in existence, as not all of the trades and industries have been nationalized or controlled by the system, but the ring is getting closer every day and pretty soon everybody will have to get out and dig, as he or she or it, are ordered or else die of hunger or a sailor or Red Guard bullet, if too strong a protest is expressed. Trotsky has often stated that nothing will stop them in the execution of their program and as practically the entire army is back of the Bolshevik movement now, there is every reason to believe in their success.

The whole attitude of the Soviet government at the peace negotiations was that of complete confidence in the success of their theories, not only in Russia, but also in all other countries, as the laboring and oppressed masses everywhere would follow their example and overthrow the present ruling classes and form one great world Democracy. This confidence has prompted them to refuse any terms, except such as were in accord with their program and they even threatened to declare a Holy War against Germany and her allies if they refuse to grant them these terms. The negotiations have been again broken off now for ten days and the question of free self-definition in

---

[7] Matvei I. Skobelev (1885–1938) was a Menshevik leader in the Petrograd Soviet and later minister of labor in the Provisional Government. After the revolution, he fled to Paris, then returned after several years, joined the Bolshevik Party, and worked with the Soviet government until his execution during Stalin's purges.

[8] Irakli Tsereteli (1881–1960) was a Georgian revolutionary who worked in the Petrograd Soviet and the Provisional Government in the months leading up to the revolution. After the revolution, Bolshevik orders for his arrest caused him to flee to Georgia. When the Soviets invaded Georgia in 1921, he fled to Paris.

the parts of Russia occupied by the enemy, as Trotsky would not go on with the negotiations until this was finally and satisfactorily settled. He is certainly completely aware of the weakness of the Russian front, although what is left cannot by any means be called a front. There is nothing left now to hinder the Germans in case they want to advance into Russia. Still the Bolsheviks refuse to acknowledge that they are the weaker side, that they are practically at the mercy of the Germans and in their negotiations are all the time in the lead and have not conceded to the Germans anything which is important according to their ideas. Whether they will be able to form that Volunteer Socialist Army of which they speak now so much it is impossible to say; in spite of all prophecies they have succeeded up to the present time. Along the internal front their forces are gaining all the time. Kiev is now surrounded by a close ring of Bolshevik troops, their ideas are rapidly converting the Ukrainians and young Cossacks to their banners. The latter now are not able to think of active warfare against the Bolsheviks; the best they can do is to hold their own ground and even that is getting more and more doubtful every day.

At present the Bolshevik government is interested to be recognized by the Allies, but in case they refuse to do so now it is certain they will have to do so later. Although taking an attitude of indifference as far as the other governments are concerned, it is actively trying to become popular with the laboring classes and soldiers of the other countries and expresses the conviction that they will either force their ruling classes to grant them the liberties the Russians have or else be thrown out. Russian Bolshevism is extremely active and aggressive. It does not intend to limit its scope of activity to Russia, it wants to dominate the whole world. This is its principal danger, as the other countries will have to either *crush* it or else to reshape themselves to the Russian pattern—there is nothing to choose between two extremes. The Russian problem will become the greatest the world ever has seen, even the German militarism will seem a small thing beside it. It will seek to change us all into citizens of the world, submitting without murmur to the dictatorship of one class, without individuality or chances to shape our own destinies, following a certain path determined for each of us by a force we dare not oppose. We shall be puppets without home, or country, or faith.

INDEX

Alekseyev, Mikhail 74, 74n1
American Lazaret xii, 17, 17n13, 21, 33, 38, 41, 77, 93, 101, 108, 118
Anderson, Henry Watkins 111, 111n16, 111n18
Avksentiev, Nikolai 144, 144n6

ballet xii, xiii, 17, 46, 76, 79, 87, 94, 105, 105n6, 106, 110
Batalha-Reis, Jaime 130, 130n3
Berkman, Alexander 56, 56n7
Billings, Warren K. 56, 56n8
Bonch-Bruyevich, Vladimir D. 86, 86n5
Breshko-Breshkovskaya, Ekaterina 144, 144n5
Brusilov, Aleksei 53, 53n6

Chernov, Victor 144, 144n4
Constitutional Democrats (Kadets) 25, 26, 84, 144
Corse, Frederick 6, 6n4, 77, 97, 128, 130, 131
Cossacks 17, 18, 19, 26, 34, 37, 38, 46, 47, 48, 49, 52, 62, 65, 73, 74, 79, 80, 89, 99, 110, 113, 121, 136, 146

Dukhonin, Nikolai N. 95, 95n1

Eloranta, Frans Evert 131, 131n4

Farwell, Mildred 109, 109n8
food x, xi, xiv, xv, 6, 8, 9, 12, 13, 15, 16, 18, 21, 25, 29, 30, 34, 36, 37, 38, 39, 40, 42, 43, 44, 46, 51, 52, 53, 54, 59, 60, 61, 65, 69, 70, 71, 75, 76, 77, 80, 82, 84, 87, 91, 94, 100, 101, 104, 107, 109, 113, 116, 117, 122, 123, 125, 127, 128, 129, 131, 132, 133
Francis, David R. 6n4, 17, 17n12, 111

Gaylord, Franklin 21, 21n16

Glennon, James H. 33, 33n1
Goldman, Emma 56, 56n7
Guchkov, A. I. 22, 22n17, 23, 28, 53

Hermitage 88
Hildebrandt, Vera Ixkull von 101, 101n5

Kadets. *See* Constitutional Democrats
Kaledin, Aleksei 111, 111n15, 121
Kalpashnikov, Andrei 110, 110n14, 111, 112, 113, 116, 123
Karsavina, Tamara 105, 105n6
Kerensky, Alexander 22n17, 27, 27n26, 41, 47, 49, 53, 61, 61n10, 65, 73, 74, 75, 76, 81, 85, 89, 96, 97, 99, 100, 123, 142, 144, 144nn5–6
Kokoshkin, Fyodor F. 119, 119n22
Kolchak, Alexander 34, 34n2, 35, 50
Kornilov, Lavr G. viii, 53, 53n5, 65, 67, 71–74, 74n2, 75, 80, 89, 99, 102
Krylenko, Nikolai V. 69, 86, 86n6
Krymov, Alexander 74, 74n2

Lenin, Vladimir I. viii, xiii, xvi, xvii, 27n26, 45, 46, 49, 53, 53n3, 86, 86nn5–6, 95n1, 99, 101, 112, 114n19, 115, 137, 144n3
Lvov, Georgy 27, 27n24, 73, 80

Maydell, Eveline Adelheid von 88, 88n7, 119
McCully, Newton A. ix, xvi, 11, 11n2, 12, 21
Milyukov, Pavel 28, 28n28
Mooney, Thomas 56, 56n8
Morgan, J. P. 139, 139n1, 140
Morris, Ira Nelson 126, 126n1, 133

Nekrasov, Nikolai V. 27, 27n25
Nicholas II vii, 11n4, 14, 15n7, 19, 20, 20n15, 22, 22nn17–18, 23, 23n20, 26, 27, 27n24, 28n28, 43, 47n2, 53, 58, 61, 64, 113, 136

Noulens, Joseph 91, 91n8

opera 12, 13, 71, 76, 79, 91, 94, 105, 110, 110nn10–11, 110n13

Pankhurst, Emmeline 35, 35n3, 41
Perkins, Roger 111, 111n17
prices and inflation 16, 18, 34, 40, 51, 58, 59, 69, 70, 82, 84, 88, 89, 95, 105, 116, 121
Provisional Government vii, viii, 11, 11n4, 26, 34, 46, 47, 48, 50, 54, 67, 68, 69, 78, 94, 98, 99, 102, 104, 113, 114, 119, 141, 142, 143

Rasputin, Grigory 15, 15n10, 20n15
Red Cross 31, 49, 50, 58, 73, 91, 109n8, 110, 111, 119
Rodzianko, Mikhail 20, 20n15, 53
Root Commission 26n23, 31, 33–42, 43, 54, 61, 65
Root, Elihu 26, 26n23, 33, 38, 43

Scavenius, Harald 123, 123n23
servants xi, xiii, xiv, 24, 30, 39, 45, 80, 95, 102, 104, 109, 109n9, 114, 118
    changed attitude of xiii, xiv, 95, 109
Shaliapin, Fyodor 110, 110n10
Shingarev, Andrei I. 119, 119nn21–22
Shulgin, Vasily 22, 22n18
Skobelev, Matvei I. 145, 145n7
Smith, L. McAllister 37, 37n4, 43, 46, 63, 126, 130, 131
soldiers, Russian vii, viii, xii, 5, 6, 7, 8, 13, 17, 18, 19, 25, 27, 28, 31, 35, 38, 39, 40, 41, 42, 43, 44, 45, 47, 48, 50, 52, 57, 58, 59, 60, 62, 67, 68, 69, 72, 74, 75, 77, 78, 81, 83, 84, 85, 87, 88, 91, 97, 98, 101, 106, 107, 112, 115, 119, 121, 127
    changed attitude of xii, xiii, xiv, 7, 8–9, 31, 58, 59, 67, 69, 81, 85, 87, 106, 127
    compared to children 5, 8, 9, 31, 40, 72, 103, 136
    officers xiii, 5, 6, 7, 8, 19, 20, 22, 23, 25, 28, 29, 30, 35, 37, 42, 44, 45, 46, 48, 50, 58, 61, 62, 65, 66, 67, 68, 69, 75, 77, 91
Spiridonova, Maria 144, 144n2
Stanley, Victor 76, 76n3
Steinberg, Isaac Nachman 144, 144n3
Stevens, John F. 98, 98n4
Stürmer, Boris 15, 15nn8–9

Tereshchenko, Mikhail 27, 27n27
Trepov, Alexander 15, 15n9
Trotsky, Leon viii, 99, 108, 112, 114n19, 115, 122, 137, 141, 142, 145, 146
Tsereteli, Irakli 145, 145n8

violence xii, 16, 18, 20, 23, 28, 30, 37, 39, 41, 42, 50, 54, 58, 62, 65, 67, 68, 71, 75, 77, 78, 80, 87, 91, 94, 95, 98, 101, 104, 106, 109, 116, 118, 119, 120, 121, 123, 135

White Guard xv, 9, 9n6, 34n2, 50, 53n5, 127, 129, 131, 132
Winship, North 12, 12n5, 17, 49
Winter Palace viii, xiv, 33, 49, 63, 93, 94, 96, 97, 106, 107
Wright, Joshua Butler 17, 17n11

YMCA 21, 49, 50

www.ingramcontent.com/pod-product-compliance
Lightning Source LLC
Chambersburg PA
CBHW032027230426
43671CB00005B/221